GOLDEN RETRIEVER

A Dog Training Guide on How to Raise, Train and Discipline Your Golden Retriever Puppy for Beginners

Joseph Lint

GOLDEN RETRIEVER

© Copyright 2020 - All rights reserved.

The content contained within this book may not be reproduced, duplicated or transmitted without direct written permission from the author or the publisher.

Under no circumstances will any blame or legal responsibility be held against the publisher, or author, for any damages, reparation, or monetary loss due to the information contained within this book. Either directly or indirectly.

Legal Notice:

This book is copyright protected. This book is only for personal use. You cannot amend, distribute, sell, use, quote or paraphrase any part, or the content within this book, without the consent of the author or publisher.

Disclaimer Notice:

Please note the information contained within this document is for educational and entertainment purposes only. All effort has been executed to present accurate, up to date, and reliable, complete information. No warranties of any kind are declared or implied. Readers acknowledge that the author is not engaging in the rendering of legal, financial, medical or professional advice. The content within this book has been derived from various sources. Please consult a licensed professional before attempting any techniques outlined in this book.

GOLDEN RETRIEVER

By reading this document, the reader agrees that under no circumstances is the author responsible for any losses, direct or indirect, which are incurred as a result of the use of information contained within this document, including, but not limited to, — errors, omissions, or inaccuracies.

GOLDEN RETRIEVER

Table of Contents

Introduction vi

Chapter One - Is A Golden Retriever A Good Fit For You? 1

Chapter Two - Choosing Your Golden Retriever 17

Chapter Three - Setting Up The Perfect Environment 27

Chapter Four - Grooming Your Golden Retriever 44

Chapter Five - Keeping Your Golden Retriever Healthy 74

Chapter Six - Training Your Golden Retriever 106

Chapter Seven - How To Discipline Your Golden Retriever 124

Chapter Eight - Timeline Of A Golden Retriever 133

Final Words 144

GOLDEN RETRIEVER

INTRODUCTION

There is an old saying that a dog is a man's best friend. If this is true, then golden retrievers surely deserve a special mention. They are friends who are so loyal and good-hearted that they look after us when we're sick and share their love with us when we're upset. Indeed, if you are looking to purchase a dog in order to have a companion, then a golden retriever should be at the top of the list for breeds to consider.

Golden retrievers have been trained to help hunters because of their heightened sense of smell. This ability has also led to their use in helping law enforcement officers track drugs and other contraband substances. This sense of smell has helped them in identifying certain medical conditions. They are very friendly and loving, their natural compassion making them a fantastic choice for help in therapy and other assistance roles such as seeing-eye dogs. They are able to work across these varied fields because they are obedient and intelligent, two features which (when combined with their compassion) make them excellent additions to any family or household that can provide the time, space, and energy to look after them.

In this book, you will learn all about these amazing canines. We'll begin by looking at the history and traits of golden retrievers to see what we can find out about the many pros and cons that come with raising them. From there, we will move into the specifics of the breed, and introduce the three types of golden retrievers. We'll see where they come from, how they differ from each other, and what size you can expect each to grow to.

Size is an important factor to keep in mind when raising a puppy because they don't stay small forever. You will need to make sure that you have enough space to care for your dog's needs. This is why we'll spend chapter three looking at the difference between raising a golden retriever in an apartment versus a house. We'll also discuss how well these puppies accept spending time alone at home while you're out at work. We'll see whether or not you'll need to hire a dogsitter.

If you can provide a loving home for your golden retriever, then you'll want to pay attention to chapter four to learn how to groom your puppy, how to give them baths, how to trim them as needed, and how to prepare for the inevitable shed hair that always seems to end up everywhere! Chapter five moves from taking care of the dog's hygiene to taking care of its health, and covers issues like lifespan, ear infections, diseases, getting enough exercise, and dietary concerns.

GOLDEN RETRIEVER

Golden retrievers are among the most obedient of dog breeds, and so you are probably going to want to know how you can train yours to stay off the couch and be on its best behavior. We'll cover this in chapter six, including how to teach them basic commands and the use of clicker training. Training naturally brings up issues of discipline, and so chapter seven will show how we can use positive reinforcement to train our golden retrievers far easier and in a healthier manner than using negative punishments.

Finally, we'll close out the book on a timeline that shows the stages of a golden retriever's life from a puppy to an adolescent, and on through adulthood. This timeline will provide a bird's eye view of the stages you will experience when you adopt a golden retriever as a loving part of your family.

CHAPTER ONE

IS A GOLDEN RETRIEVER A GOOD FIT FOR YOU?

Bringing a dog into your family is a big decision. You need to consider their needs (space, exercise, diet, socialization) to weigh whether or not you are able to provide for them properly. Many of us begged our parents for a dog when we were young, only to never actually get one. Heartbreaking as it was as a kid, it is easy to look back and see how our living situations wouldn't have been good for a dog. Despite our childhood disappointment, we can see how our parents made the right decision.

In this chapter, you will be given enough information to determine if a golden retriever is a good fit for your home. Issues of size and diet will come later as we get into more specifics. For now, we'll take a look at the history of these remarkable canines to see how they got their reputation. We'll examine what traits and characteristics are shared across the breed, and both the pros and the cons of choosing a golden retriever. By the end, you should have enough information to decide if a golden retriever is the right breed for your household or not.

The History of the Golden Retriever

Historical evidence tells us that dogs have been humanity's best friend for over 30,000 years. Yet, despite this, golden retrievers can only trace their history back to the 1800s. This is relatively nothing in the grand scale of canine development. But it actually tells us something very interesting. Despite such a short history, golden retrievers are considered one of the best breeds there are. While other breeds have a much longer history, the golden retriever shows us that it isn't about how long you have been around, but rather how much of an impact you can make. When it comes to the world of canines, golden retrievers have made the biggest of splashes.

Believe it or not, the first reference of a golden retriever in written form comes from the journals of Lord Tweedmouth in Scotland. The golden furred retriever in question was named Nous, the only brightly colored dog in a litter of black-furred puppies. Lord Tweedmouth decided to breed Nous, and so he chose a tweed water spaniel named Belle. This origin story wouldn't be a bad idea for a Disney story of its own, as this union is responsible for all of the golden retrievers in the world today.

By the start of the Twentieth Century, the world at large hadn't been introduced to these dogs. Lord Tweedmouth had kept the existence of this new breed of retriever between himself and his fellow noblemen. As they were being selectively bred, traits from water spaniels, Irish setters, and other retrievers were introduced into the golden retriever. By 1908, they were ready to be presented to a wider public, and one Lord Harcourt put on a much-publicized show with his personal hounds. It proved to be a big hit, but there was a small problem. They still didn't have a name for the breed at this time.

Lord Harcourt's exhibit was part of a larger dog show, and this meant the judges would have to categorize this new species of dog. But more than a name, they would need to decide on a class to place it under. It easily slotted under the retriever category, but there was still the issue with the name. Whether it was decided by Lord Harcourt or written by a judge, the dogs left the event with the name "golden retriever," and the public has known them as such ever since.

The Traits and Characteristics of Golden Retrievers

Golden retrievers make for fantastic pets and work dogs. Part of this is because of their strong physical traits. But another part, arguably the biggest, is the intellectual and emotional characteristics they exhibit as well. We'll begin with the physical and then move on to the emotional afterward.

Male golden retrievers typically weigh between 65 and 75 pounds, with females usually being around ten pounds lighter when they aren't pregnant. The males also tend to be a little taller, generally two feet or so, while the females are a couple of inches less. Their fur is considered to be medium-length and is usually straight. Some golden retrievers will have fur so yellow in places that it looks white, but, typically, they are entirely made up of different shades of yellow. Their coats are good at keeping water off. The aristocrats who bred the species were interested in hunting waterfowl, so it would make sense they would aim for a water-resistant fur that helps the hounds swim. A strong nose for tracking was also a must.

Of course, these days, the breed isn't used for hunting so much. You are more likely to see them working as search and rescue dogs, seeing-eye dogs for the blind, or comfort dogs working with children's hospitals. Somehow, despite the fact that their origins began in hunting, golden retrievers are one of the most compassionate, loyal, and obedient dog breeds there are. It is these features that make them the perfect choice for people looking for a friendly companion for themselves or their children.

One of the reasons that golden retrievers are so beloved is they love to cuddle. If you are the type to hug your pets (and who out there among us isn't?), then a golden retriever is a good fit because they love hugs. They love pleasing their owners, and this helps to make training them much easier. They're also absolutely fantastic around children because they are very gentle dogs despite their history. They don't bark a lot naturally, but younger golden retrievers can be excitable and loud.

They can be trained out of it, though. But, if you are looking for a guard dog, then they're a bad pick; a golden retriever is so friendly they'll probably hold onto a burglar's flashlight rather than bark to alert you about them! They get along with pretty much anyone, and are even suitable for households with other pets. They're adorable little furballs that are utterly devoted to their owners. It should be no surprise why they are beloved members of so many households all over the globe.

Pros and Cons: Introduction

Adopting a puppy is a big choice. There are many different breeds you could choose, and they all have their strengths and weaknesses. Golden retrievers are no different this way. They have a lot of pros, but they also have some cons. After this, we'll weigh both sides to get an accurate answer to whether or not a golden retriever is the best idea for you.

The Pros

Their Calm Nature: A golden retriever is one of the most gentle and calm breeds there are. They might not start out that way. Puppies can be quite a handful at first, but as these dogs mature, they become more and more relaxed. They have a sense of noble pride and are very grandmotherly in the way they care for the family members around them. They take well to living with other pets, and you'll often find them taking care of younger dogs. They aren't prone to violence; they're more likely to help a mouse steal some crackers than they are to catch it.

They are Easy to Train: There is a reason that golden retrievers are one of the go-to breeds used in service work. They are intelligent and incredibly obedient. They can be trained to support a person through their entire day, helping to fetch slippers, or reminding patients about medicine they need to take. They are remarkably bright, and they are loyal to a fault, and so they use that intelligence to learn tricks and behavior that will please their owners. Not only are they quick to learn, they *like* to learn because hearing "good boy" or "good girl" means the world to them. Plus, knowing they'll get a treat or two doesn't hurt either, of course!

They are Happy to Meet New People: Some dogs get nervous in large gatherings. They need a room to hide in, or they'll retreat to the yard. But golden retrievers adore meeting new people, and they're delighted to be surrounded by lots of friendly faces. Golden retrievers don't think of themselves as the family dog, they think of themselves as one of the family. They want to be with its members as much as possible, and they certainly expect to be called to any family meetings that are scheduled.

They Like to Meet New Pets: If you live in a household with a lot of pets, then you have probably encountered that dreaded moment when a new furry addition gets in a fight with your other pets. Claws and teeth start going, and it can take weeks or months to integrate them into the household. Sometimes, it never works. Thankfully, you seldom hear this about golden retrievers. On the other hand, you do hear about golden retrievers who become the best friend to other dogs, bunnies, cats, ferrets, pigs, sheep, and more. These dogs truly love, and can bond with creatures of any species. It's like there's enough love in their heart for everything they encounter.

GOLDEN RETRIEVER

They Stay Playful: While older golden retrievers fall into more grandparent-style habits, younger golden retrievers act like puppies for years. They learn how to behave better, but when played with, they will be as energetic and youthful as a dog half their age. Together with their compassionate nature, this makes a golden retriever a great fit for a household with children. However, there is a flip side to this particular pro that we'll be looking at shortly.

They're Quiet: As mentioned, a golden retriever is a terrible pick for a guard dog. While they may start out barking a bit while they are younger, they very quickly grow into quite quiet creatures.

GOLDEN RETRIEVER

The Cons

They're Large Dogs: As noted, the males will grow to be up to 75 pounds, and that's a lot of dog. A growing puppy needs lots of food, but a 75-pound dog needs more. But you've got to be careful with a golden retriever. They will keep eating and eating if you put food in front of them, and an obese golden retriever is the result. You do need to be mindful of how much food they are given.

They Need to Workout: Just like you or me need to exercise in order to stay healthy, a golden retriever needs exercise as well. They have lots of energy, and they really need to get out and use all of their muscles. That means that you need to take them out for an hour a day. But just walking them isn't enough. It's better than nothing, but what's ideal is a good run. Something that lets them work their muscles hard for an hour. They're physical dogs, and without their exercise, they can start to get restless and anxious. Plus, an out of shape dog is much more likely to be an overweight dog.

They Need Company: Golden retrievers are great with large families. They're less great with being left alone for most of the day. They need to be around living, breathing people. Some people think that all they need to do is turn on a radio or a TV and their dog will be fine, but this simply isn't true. They need to have real company, or they will get depressed and restless.

So Much Shedding: During the spring and fall, you are going to get used to having a lot of dog hair over everything. They might only have medium length hair, but their coats are thick, and shedding their winter and summer coats produces what is commonly referred to as a "hair explosion." We'll be learning more about this in chapter four, but this particular con makes golden retrievers a bad idea for households that need to be concerned about pet allergies.

At Risk for Health Problems: As with any breed, there are certain health problems that seem to strike golden retrievers quite often. These include issues such as hip dysplasia, which is an unfortunately common problem. Other frequent concerns are cataracts on their eyes, and even vision-related neuro issues such as epilepsy. Also, they're prone to progressive retinal atrophy, subvalvular aortic stenosis, osteochondritis dissecans, osteosarcoma, hemangiosarcoma, and gastric dilatation volvulus. Plus, as if they needed another thing to worry about, golden retrievers also tend to develop a bunch of allergies.

Pros versus Cons: The Outcome

GOLDEN RETRIEVER

The pros pretty much speak for themselves. These are loving, intelligent, gentle beasts who want nothing more than to make their owners happy and to feel like a part of a loving family. They fit well into almost any household dynamic, but their pros might indicate the limits of what you will need to be able to provide.

If you are just getting by in terms of income, then you should reconsider getting a golden retriever until you are positive that you can provide it with enough food. They are very much big puppies in terms of their personalities, after all. You should also be able to afford visits with the vet in case your golden retriever faces any of the health problems that are so common in the breed. This again suggests that you should consider if you have enough money to care for them if the worst-case scenario were to occur.

But money isn't enough. You can't expect to leave a golden retriever at home alone while you work all day. You need to be able to give it company, either by being nearby or by getting a dog sitter to look after it. You also need to be able to provide it with plenty of exercise. That means you need to be present and a big part of your dog's life. If you can't be around enough to help it grow and take care of its mental and physical health, then you may want to consider a less demanding breed.

Finally, you need to be okay with the fact that there is going to be dog hair on everything. Even the most closely followed grooming advice won't prevent dog hair from spreading when it's the season for shedding. If you have people in your household who are allergic to dog hair, or if cleanliness is a major concern of yours, then a golden retriever might not be right for you.

But if you have enough money to provide a golden retriever with proper food and attention to its physical health, plus enough time and attention to bond with it and make it feel like a part of the family, then they are one of the most loyal, intelligent, and rewarding dogs that you could ever ask for. They make perfect additions to nearly every home and every family, and they have an unlimited amount of love inside their furry little bodies that they'll want to share with you.

GOLDEN RETRIEVER

Chapter Summary

- Adding a golden retriever to your life is a big deal; it's important to carefully consider this decision to be sure you can properly tend for a new dog.

- While humanity and dogs have been friends for centuries, golden retrievers were only discovered and bred into existence as a strain of their own in the late 1800s.

- Golden retrievers were bred for gentlemanly sports such as hunting waterfowl.

- The public wasn't introduced to golden retrievers until 1908 when Lord Harcourt showed off his personal kennel.

- Golden retrievers are beautiful, intelligent dogs with medium-length coats. They weigh up to between 65 and 75 pounds when they are adults and stand about two feet tall.

- Golden retrievers have strong muscles and noses, plus a coat that naturally repels water. These were all features that made them ideal for hunting waterfowl, where they would need to trudge through swamps and woods.

- You can find golden retrievers working as seeing-eye dogs, police sniffers, or comfort dogs in children's hospitals or college campuses.

GOLDEN RETRIEVER

There are many jobs that golden retrievers can be trained to learn because of their intelligence.

- This breed is also highly notable for their loyalty, compassion, and obedience. Golden retrievers develop deep bonds with their humans, and they strive to please them. They are eager to learn commands and impress their owners. They are also filled with so much love that they make for wonderful pets if you are considering adding a dog to a family with children.

- These adorable fluff-balls also love to cuddle and be patted, meet new people, and be around their family.

- There are a lot of great pros to adding a golden retriever to your family. They have a calm nature and often grow into very peaceful adults; they take well to training and can learn a lot of commands; they love meeting new people; they love meeting new pets; they stay playful even as they get older, and they're one of the quieter breeds around.

- There are also a few cons. Golden retrievers are large dogs, and so they take up a lot of space; they need to get plenty of exercise because they have a lot of muscles; they don't do well being left alone for long stretches; they shed a lot of hair, and they are prone to developing health problems which keep their expected life spans shorter.

GOLDEN RETRIEVER

- If you are considering getting a dog, then the pros outweigh the cons, so long as you can provide enough attention to your golden retriever to train it and avoid leaving it home alone for hours. You will also want to have enough money for medical costs in case of emergency or health issues.

In the next chapter, you will learn how to choose the type of golden retriever that is right for you. There are three types: Canadian golden retrievers, American golden retrievers, and British golden retrievers. We'll look at each to see what traits they share and where they differ. We'll also take a moment to consider the size of these dogs and what that tells us about caring for them.

CHAPTER TWO

CHOOSING YOUR GOLDEN RETRIEVER

Once you have decided that a golden retriever is the right fit for your household, you still need to actually choose the puppy that you are going to be raising. Even though you have decided to get a golden retriever, you still have another choice that needs to be made. You still need to decide what *type* of golden retriever you want. There are three to choose from, each with their notable features.

Assuming that you are getting your golden retriever as a puppy and not a full-grown dog, you will want to consider how the dog is going to fill out as it gets older. There are some tricks that you can use to get an idea of how large your puppy is going to be so that you can choose a golden retriever that's the right size for your living space. By the end of this chapter, you'll be equipped with the knowledge you need to pick the perfect new addition to your family.

The Three Types of Golden Retriever

There is an English golden retriever, a Canadian golden retriever, and an American golden retriever. The differences between these types are almost entirely down to their physical appearance. "Under the hood," as it were, they are the same dog. This means they are prone to the same illnesses, but they are also full of the same vast amount of love that their breed is known for. We'll look at each one of these types to get a sense of what makes them special and unique when compared to the other types.

GOLDEN RETRIEVER

American Golden Retriever: The American golden retriever isn't as large as the Canadian version, but they are on a par with the British golden retriever. Though roughly the same size, American golden retrievers have longer torsos than their cousins. They typically have much less muscle mass than other types. Their fur is about the same size as the British golden retriever's, but it is usually a shade darker. The American golden retriever most often has light-colored eyes, which is one of the ways it stands out. It also has a triangular-shaped skull that flares out from the front.

British Golden Retriever: The British golden retriever has the most recognizable traits of the golden retriever. Perhaps that's not surprising considering the breed came out of Scotland. They aren't as large as the Canadian golden retriever, and, in fact, they are often smaller than even the American breed. However, you might not be able to tell a British golden retriever apart from an American since they can be the same size, and their coats are of similar length. Not only that, but they behave with just as much love as their American or Canadian cousins. The main way to tell a British golden retriever apart is the way they are shaped, with a big

GOLDEN RETRIEVER

broad skull and strong front legs. You will also find that the British bred tend to have darker eyes than the others.

Canadian Golden Retriever: The Canadian golden retriever stands out from the American or British types, and it is very easy to tell them apart when they're together. While the American and British types have medium-length hair that grows in waves, the Canadian animal has much shorter hair that doesn't grow as thick. While this makes them look like smaller dogs, they are taller than either the British or American varieties, and this makes up for their smaller coats.

Selecting the Right Sized Golden Retriever

As we discussed in the last chapter, a male golden retriever grows up to 75 pounds and the females up to 65. Of course, overfeeding a golden retriever will end up with overweight dogs that could push 100 pounds. This is very unhealthy for your dog, plus expensive for your pocketbook, so let's stick to proper feeding and take 75 pounds as the standard. Of course, this isn't how much a puppy weighs. They're so soft and tiny, it can be hard to picture how your golden retriever puppy could become such a big dog, but it happens. In fact, it happens in only a year and a half, and so your small dog will become a big dog quicker than you'd imagine.

When you first select a puppy, if you are purchasing or adopting, then you are probably going to be looking at a single litter. That is, one mother's babies. These fluffy little brothers and sisters could all be the same size, or there could be fast growers or runts in a litter. These might make for the cutest puppies, but this could also be a sign that the dog is going to have health issues throughout its life due to its improper growth. In general, you are going to want to pick a puppy of normal size.

A golden retriever puppy shouldn't be taken away from its mother until it is at least eight weeks old. It can be later than eight weeks, but it should never be earlier. At this stage, when the puppies are ready for a new home, they should be about ten pounds. This is a good range, but, bear in mind, they can be up to five times this weight in less than a year. They are one of the faster-growing dogs, and you can expect them to be full height in less than a year, at which point they will start to get wider as their muscle develops and they fill out. So when you look at that puppy, you need to remember that in a week, it is going to be nearly twice the weight. It is going to grow fast.

If you are looking for a smaller dog, then you should select a female. In addition to being ten pounds lighter than a male, the females are several inches shorter as well. Select an English golden retriever for a smaller build as well. Selecting a regular-sized puppy will allow you to be able to predict the growth of the dog into adulthood, at which point the female will be a little bit smaller. But a full-grown golden retriever is still going to be about two feet tall and over 50 pounds, even at the small end of the scale.

GOLDEN RETRIEVER

GOLDEN RETRIEVER

Chapter Summary

- While golden retrievers start small, they grow into big dogs. It is important that you consider the puppy you are adopting carefully.

- There are three types of golden retriever: the American, British, and Canadian breeds. These three types are all golden retrievers, so they aren't all that different from each other, but they each have their unique qualities.

- The American golden retriever is about the same size as the British one. They have longer torsos than the other kinds, as well as about the same, or even less, muscle mass. American golden retrievers have fur that is a little darker than the British variety, and eyes that are lighter in color. American golden retrievers also have a triangular-shaped skull.

- British golden retrievers are often just slightly smaller than the American type. They have similar coats, but big, broad skulls and very powerful front legs. They also have much darker eyes than the other two breeds.

- Canadian golden retrievers have a coat of fur that is shorter than either the American or British. This makes them look like smaller dogs and helps them to stand out from their cousins.

- A golden retriever will grow to be 65 to 75 pounds if it is male, and 55 to 65 if it is female.

GOLDEN RETRIEVER

- Overweight golden retrievers can be up to 100 pounds.

- Puppies will begin light and put on a few pounds each week until they get to full weight.

- When looking to adopt a puppy, it might seem like a good idea to pick the runt of the litter. They are often the cutest. But this can be a sign of potential health issues as the golden retriever gets older. You will have fewer potential problems if you stick to a normal-sized puppy.

- A golden retriever should be two months old, at least before it is taken away from its mother. At this point, they should be ten pounds.

- Golden retrievers will be full height within a year, and maximum weight in between a year to two years. They start out small and adorable. They may stay adorable, but they will get big real quick.

In the next chapter, you will learn how to prepare your home for a golden retriever. We'll look at the difference between raising a golden retriever in an apartment versus a house, and how well they handle being left alone throughout the day to see whether or not you will need to hire a dogsitter.

CHAPTER THREE

SETTING UP THE PERFECT ENVIRONMENT

Once you have selected a puppy, you are going to need to bring that puppy home. But you should really take a few minutes and consider whether you can offer a healthy living space for a golden retriever. Bringing a dog into a bad living environment is never a good idea, and it almost guarantees that you will face many issues relating to the dog's physical and mental wellbeing.

In this chapter, we will ask the big question that is on many reader's minds: If I live in an apartment, can I still raise a golden retriever? With the rise of urban living, more and more people are living in apartments, and that means more pets are as well. We'll see if a golden retriever can be raised in apartments before turning our attention towards leaving them alone, and how we can fit a work schedule around our new puppy. Finally, we'll look at ways we can prepare to bring a puppy into our lives and our homes to smooth out the transition.

Can I Raise a Golden Retriever in an Apartment?

The short answer is yes. But the long answer is that while you can raise a golden retriever to be perfectly healthy and happy in an apartment, you are going to need to dedicate more time and attention to them to make up for this fact. There will be limitations you can't escape from. So let's start with the basics.

Golden retrievers grow up to 75 pounds, and so this means you have a big heavy dog. This requires enough space for an animal of this size to turn around and maneuver. If you are in an overcrowded apartment, or one that is particularly small, then you aren't going to be able to provide this room. Even if you can provide the room, you are going to need to make sure that there is nothing breakable that can be knocked over or fall down. You are bringing an exuberant mass of muscle and energy into your home and things will happen.

However, remember that golden retrievers take very well to training. You can teach a golden retriever how to move around a limited space, and you can even teach them how to help you with your daily routines like waking up the kids or getting ready for work in the morning. This is terrific because it provides you with a helpful companion, rather than just an adorable and furry distraction. Listen, we all love our cats, but they're not going to bring us our slippers any time soon!

Golden retrievers don't do well when they have to stay alone for long periods. This is true regardless of where they live, but it is especially true when they live in a small apartment. One of the things you should do when you bring a golden retriever home to a small apartment is to take it around the neighborhood to give it lots of different sights and smells. If you bring it into a small apartment without doing this, then it will get quite lonely and sad. They like company, and they like smells, and your apartment probably won't offer much of either. If you keep a golden retriever in an apartment, then you should be coming home to spend time with it more often than you would the same dog in a bigger house.

One of the reasons you should come back more often to spend time with your golden retriever is its boundless energy. When living in a smaller space, golden retrievers need more vigorous exercise to stay in shape. You will need to walk and run with your dog more when living in an apartment, but this can be a bonus benefit to your health as well as the dog's.

If you are able to come home more often to give your golden retriever the attention it needs, then you should be able to raise your pet just fine in an apartment. They are obedient and can be trained to fit well into a smaller space, even helping you out. Just make sure that you can take it outside often, or it will get depressed and anxious, and that's a horribly heartbreaking sight.

Home Alone: How Long is Too Long?

Right out the gate, we are going to set a limit of five hours alone. This isn't just for the dog's loneliness, but for the sake of your apartment or house. You shouldn't leave your golden retriever alone for more than five hours. This is because you shouldn't make your dog wait more than five hours to go to the washroom. Allowing that to happen isn't fair. You could simply stop in to check up on the dog, perhaps not enough to stop its loneliness, but enough to take care of its health. This is the absolute bare minimum that you need to be able to provide. It's not even the best, just the lowest bar you need to be able to pass before buying a golden retriever.

A golden retriever may get anxious when it is left alone, even for a short amount of time. This is more prevalent when it is younger, and this can result in unfortunate behavior. Distressed golden retrievers may damage furniture or belongings, or urinate and defecate throughout the house. A golden retriever that hasn't been house trained is far more likely to use the washroom where it isn't supposed to, but this behavior can be trained out of them while still young. While these may be signs of anxiety, they might also be signs of boredom.

Boredom and anxiety can both lead to destructive behavior, but they signify different issues the dog is facing. Boredom can be fixed with a little training and the addition of some toys for it to play with. Anxiety-based behavior will require longer training, and you'll need to offer the dog comfort and understanding while you work on the problem with them.

GOLDEN RETRIEVER

One way that people have tried to make raising a golden retriever work is to take the dog around with them throughout the day. This works fine if you are driving around and physically interacting with the dog. But some owners use a kennel to house the dog while they're away, and this is a horrible way to treat your dog. If you can't offer them enough time, then it is better not to adopt them in the first place.

However, there are some ways you can set up your living environment to make a golden retriever more comfortable so that they can go longer periods without getting lonely or bored. Those that live in a house will likely have more room to offer a golden retriever to roam around and explore. This provides more sights and smells and helps to keep boredom down. If your dog has a space to poop and pee, then it doesn't need to be let out, but this is rare. More often, you'll need to come home at least every five hours to let it out. You need to provide plenty of water for a golden retriever to drink while you are gone; they are thirsty animals. How much water and space you can provide will go a long way in determining how successfully you can leave your golden retriever at home. But there are several approaches that owners have taken to be able to leave them at home with worrying about chewed furniture. You can use one of these methods as well.

GOLDEN RETRIEVER

One approach is to leave your golden retriever with a captivating toy to play with. There are toys like the Trixie Activity Flip Book, which can keep a dog occupied for hours, trying to figure out their way through a physical puzzle to get to a treat at the end. Toys that challenge your dog's intelligence to get a treat are a fine way to train their brains while keeping them away from the furniture. If you have a golden retriever that gets bored easily, then some treat puzzles will be a good plan.

GOLDEN RETRIEVER

Many owners will claim that leaving the TV on while they are gone will help their dogs. This is both right and wrong. The people who claim it is right often say their golden retriever was always chewing the furniture until they started leaving the TV on. Others claim that their dog chews it even when the TV is on. Whether or not this will work with your dog will depend if the destructive behavior is from boredom or anxiety. If it is from boredom, then a TV left on can be a good tool to keep them distracted. But if the destructive behavior is a result of separation anxiety, then the TV isn't going to be any use; you will need to provide the dog with more physical, at-home, attention.

Another approach is to have a friend or neighbor stop by to take your dog out to use the washroom or even for a walk. You could hire a dog sitter if you are going to be gone a long time or a dog walker if you won't have a chance to take them out for their exercise. There are centers that you can drop a dog off for the day, and pick them up at night, just like a daycare you might take your children to. You can expect these to cost anywhere from $20 to several hundred dollars a month, depending on how often you need to use their services. Ultimately, it's better to go with a neighbor or friend, or to come home and spend more time with your dog. Going to a daycare center can have bad results. You can't ensure that your dog isn't being mistreated, and even when it is being treated wonderfully, it could bond with an employee, and then find themselves very sad when they aren't able to visit the daycare anymore.

Preparing for a Golden Retriever in Your Life

While you will need to prepare your home, you are also going to need to prepare your life schedule and your finances for the adorable furball you are going to be raising. By taking preliminary steps, you will be able to save lots of time, energy, and avoid frustration.

The first thing you are going to do is prepare your home. If you have children, then you should sit them down and talk to them about what it means to have a puppy. This isn't just a cute stuffed animal, but a living and breathing creature that feels love and pain just like the kids do. Make sure that you talk to your kids about puppy-proofing the home. Walk them through the steps you'll take. That will include making sure electrical cords aren't in plain sight, and that shoes and clothes are picked up and put away properly. Make sure that cupboards aren't left open, and that there aren't any foods or cleaning supplies left out in the open where a puppy could get to them. Make sure that the puppy isn't able to eat food intended for other pets like a cat. It isn't harmful to the puppy, but it will lead to overeating and one super-angry cat. You may need to be more careful when you feed your animals; leave cat food where the dog can't climb.

Once everything that you don't want your puppy to get into is out of sight, you should then start laying out and putting away any supplies you've got for the puppy. You are going to want to get a collar for the dog and a leash to take it on walks. A bowl for water and another for food should be laid out in an area designated for the dog. You'll also want to purchase some hard food for the dog, and a little bit of soft food can make for a great supper time treat or help in getting medicines down. You should also get some ID tags for the dog's collar. A doggie bed that provides a space that is entirely the dog's is an excellent idea to help with anxiety. While a puppy doesn't have much hair, getting a brush to help reduce shedding is a smart idea too. Make sure that you get chew toys and other toys for entertaining them. Puppies with chew toys quickly learn that they are okay to nibble on, and they don't go after the furniture unless there is a deeper problem.

Once everything is laid out, your new puppy can be introduced to the home. You are going to want to help the puppy get used to your home by sticking to a schedule. Routine and patterns will help the dog adjust, though you should consider these routines in depth before you create them. When you start to change a dog's routines, it gets confused and sometimes worried. Create routines that you will be able to stick to over long stretches of time. You need to feed the dog three times a day for the first three months, and puppies need to use the bathroom every couple of hours. They require more time and attention as they are growing. Stick to the same feeding times and try to stick to regular bathroom breaks. Try to sleep roughly the same time and wake at the same time as well. It may seem weird to stick to a schedule when it comes to using the bathroom, but this will help with training them to go outside.

You should be kind to your puppy when you first introduce it into the home. If it has accidents in the house or chews on something it shouldn't, don't get too angry. They don't know the rules yet, and they are still learning. They don't yet know where they belong in the world or how everything works, but they are eager to learn. They're excited to be a part of the family, but you need to be respectful of the fact that they are dogs. They need to chew, so provide chew toys. They need to learn how to go outside; it doesn't come naturally to them. But they are fast learners, so it won't be any problem as long as you respect how young they are at this stage.

Given a schedule to follow, your golden retriever should be able to start integrating into the family life quite quickly. Once they understand that the home is theirs as well, that they are a valued member of the family, they will be eager to make you happy. They learn quickly, so early mistakes aren't likely to be repeated. When there are repeated mistakes such as damaged furniture, look to see if it is from boredom or anxiety and treat accordingly. Also, don't be surprised if your golden retriever sleeps a lot. Puppies are such energetic little creatures, and all the hopping and running around tires them out. You shouldn't be surprised if your puppy sleeps for 18 hours a day. It takes a lot of beauty sleep to be that adorable after all.

GOLDEN RETRIEVER

Chapter Summary

- Introducing a puppy to the home is no small task. You need to be ready for a puppy by removing anything that might hurt them or that they might break. Remember that a puppy is following its instincts, and it doesn't know anything until you train it. If you forgot to put away that priceless vase in the living room, it isn't the puppy's fault when it breaks.

- It is important to consider if we can provide a healthy living space for our golden retrievers. We should never bring a puppy into an environment that can't support it.

- It is possible to raise a golden retriever in an apartment and keep it healthy and happy. But it will take more time and effort on your part.

- Golden retrievers are big animals, and so you need to think about how much space there is for a dog. Remember that puppies grow quickly, so you may find that what was more than enough room for a puppy isn't nearly enough for a full-grown golden retriever.

- Golden retrievers can be trained in depth, and this can make it easier to live with your pet in a tight space when compared to other breeds of similar size.

- Golden retrievers don't do well when they are left alone for long periods. In an apartment, this is even more true, since there is even less space for the dog to find entertainment.

- When bringing a golden retriever to live in a small space, it is helpful to let them see that the world outside of the apartment is big, loud, and filled with all sorts of interesting smells. This will make the experience less depressing for the dog.

- Golden retrievers have lots of energy. You will find yourself needing to exercise with them and take them for longer or more frequent walks when they are cooped up inside an apartment.

- If you have a large enough apartment and are in it often enough to look after a golden retriever, then there is nothing wrong with raising one in an apartment.

- A golden retriever should not be left alone for more than five hours at a time. Beyond concerns about the dog's mental health, which are important and valid, any longer than five hours and you will find yourself coming home to find your golden retriever has had an accident since you left.

- Golden retrievers get anxious when left alone. Distressed golden retrievers may damage property.

- Damaged property may be a sign of a golden retriever with anxiety or one that is bored. If toys and entertainment take care of the damaging behavior, then boredom was the cause. If they are still showing the same behavior, then they are being left alone too long.

- Some people suggest leaving the TV on for your dog, but this just doesn't cut it. A dog can't smell and interact with the people on the TV.

- Giving your dog a space to use the bathroom and sights and smells it can take in while you are gone will allow for less anxiety and less clean up on your part.

- A toy with some hidden treats can keep a golden retriever's attention for hours.

- If you can't visit your golden retriever while you are at work, consider letting a friend or neighbor stop in to visit the dog and reassure them everything is fine. Your dog will love having a friend stop by.

- Preparing your home for a golden retriever is essential, but so is preparing your life for one. Golden retrievers require time, energy, attention, and money.

- Prepare your home for a golden retriever by talking to your family members about what it means to have a dog. Make sure that anything fragile or edible is put away where the puppy can't get at it. Slowly introduce them to other pets, and create spaces for other pets like cats to have their privacy.

GOLDEN RETRIEVER

- Purchase supplies for your puppy prior to adoption. A bowl for food and water, toys, ID tags, leash and collar, doggie bed, and food are some of the many items that you'll need for raising a golden retriever. Don't forget combs for their coat or scissors for trims.

- Dogs are most comfortable when their life fits a schedule. This is especially true when you are first introducing a puppy into your life. It is better to get a puppy at a time when you can follow a schedule to make the transition easier. If you are in a crunch period of work and always at the office at odd hours, then it isn't a great time to get a puppy.

- Following a schedule will help you with training your golden retriever as well.

In the next chapter, you will learn how to groom your golden retriever. They are quite hairy puppies who are known for shedding lots. You will learn how to prepare for this shedding, how to brush and bathe your golden retriever, and how you go about giving them a trim when the time is right, and their hair is getting shaggy.

CHAPTER FOUR

GROOMING YOUR GOLDEN RETRIEVER

Golden retrievers are big dogs with lots of fur that hangs low to the ground. It is easy to see how this can result in a lot of messes if you aren't careful. A romp through mud puddles might be a golden retriever's dream come true, but having to steam clean the family couch after a muddy dog has trampled over it isn't a whole lot of fun for us humans. In cases like this, you are going to want to know how to give your dog a bath.

We'll be covering baths in this chapter, as well as more general grooming needs such as brushing. Brushing does a lot more than make your puppy's hair straighter, and so it is an excellent idea to learn how to brush your golden retriever correctly. You'll also learn about trimming their coats and how, with some simple considerations and preparation, you can make shedding into less of a hassle. This chapter will provide you with everything you need to know to keep your golden retriever clean and beautiful.

Brushing a Golden Retriever: How and Why You Should

A golden retriever's coat may only be classified as medium-length, but anyone that has spent time with one of these dogs knows that they somehow seem to have an endless amount of fur. This is great for your dog because it offers them a ton of protection from the elements, and it helps to keep them warm, but they can get dirty really quick. A golden retriever's fur will attract dirt, grass, and dust like crazy. Considering how much exercise a golden retriever needs, they are often moving around and kicking up dirt and gunk around them. Thankfully, a golden retriever's fur prevents this from harming the dog, but if it is ignored for any length of time, then various issues with the coat can arise.

The biggest issue that happens is their fur can get matted. Matted hair can often be brushed out and saved, but when it is left untreated, it can get tangled up so badly that the only solution is to take a pair of scissors and trim away the problem. We'll learn more about trimming shortly, but in the meantime, we can help our puppies to avoid this by creating a daily brushing habit. Not every dog is going to need a daily treatment, but golden retrievers have what is called a "double coat."

This means that their fur grows in two layers rather than one. It offers the dog much more protection, with the outer hairs shielding the inner hairs from gunk. But this also increases the rate of matting and so it needs to be maintained by us owners. That means that one of the best ways we can protect our golden retriever's fur is to brush it.

But this is only one of the ways that brushing helps to keep our dogs healthy. Golden retrievers have a lot of naturally occurring oils in their fur that helps them to dry off quickly. They were bred in order to hunt waterfowl originally, and this extra oil was fantastic for a dog that was required to swim and trudge through swampy lands to catch prey. When you properly brush a golden retriever's coat, you help to spread these healthy oils throughout the fur to keep it shiny and beautiful. This same brushing will also help to prevent or work out early mats, and it will also help to knock loose any dirt and soot that has become trapped. There are a ton of great health reasons to brush your dog, but not every dog brush is built the same. We'll turn our attention to brushes in a moment, but first, let's cover the emotional and behavioral reasons for brushing your golden retriever.

GOLDEN RETRIEVER

Beginning with the emotional side, it isn't hard to see how enjoyable brushing a golden retriever is. Do you enjoy petting a dog? Then you're going to enjoy brushing one. Do you enjoy seeing happy doggos? Then you definitely are going to enjoy brushing your golden retriever. Brushing your dog is an activity that your dog will love. So, doing this not only looks out for its health, but it is also a great way to bond with your dog. Remember, too, that dogs are very much into patterns and rituals. If you usually walk them after supper, then they start to prepare for a walk as soon as you finish eating. So, if you brush your dog at the same time, your dog will learn to expect the ritual, and this can create a wonderful moment in which you can ignore the troubles of the world and spend a minute with your dog.

Spending time with your dog and teaching it to be used to being handled in this manner is a great way to prepare your dog for meeting people out in the world, such as dog walkers or vets. Brushing your dog isn't a very hard activity. You simply run a brush through their fur. But if you are going to do it completely, then you will quickly find yourself getting your dog to lift a leg so you can brush it, putting that leg down and picking up the next one. You'll need to get its tummy and its back and all 360 degrees around the neck. This isn't difficult, but it gets you into the dog's space. Doing so is going to help the dog get more comfortable with those strangers in the white room who keep poking it with thermometers and the like. If you want a dog that gets complimented for being well-behaved, then you need to train them and get them used to having people hover over them. Brushing your dog is one of the ways that you help to calm its behavior and help prepare your dog for the real world.

There are several kinds of brushes that we can choose from to keep our golden retrievers properly maintained. These include pin brushes, bristle brushes, undercoat brushes, and slicker brushes. You can get away with using a regular pin brush or a bristle brush with your golden retriever, but if there are already mats or issues with the coat, then you will want to use a slicker brush. An undercoat brush, sometimes called an undercoat rake, can be a useful tool, since it is used to help with shedding. So, if you can afford it, you should have a general brush, a mat brush, and an undercoat brush. These three will give you everything you need to look after your golden retriever. We'll look at each briefly before moving on to bathing our dogs.

For a general-purpose brush, you will want to get either a pin or a bristle brush. Either of these is going to be used for the same purpose, and so you don't need to purchase both. Ultimately, what you use for general brushing will come down to a consideration of how much each option costs and which you personally prefer. Pin brushes have evenly spaced rows of long, thin pins that flow easily through a golden retriever's coat. If you are worried that the pins may hurt your dog, then you should purchase a pin brush with plastic coverings to reduce doggy discomfort. If you go for the plastic-protected tops, then you will need to replace your brush more often. On the other hand, a bristle brush is quite similar to a pin brush, but it uses bristles instead of metal pins. Bristle brushes are better at cleaning dirt from the dog's coat, but a pin brush will be better at breaking up potential mats. A pin brush is better than a bristle brush if it is the only brush you can buy, since the pins offer a way of tackling mats. But if you are able to purchase a slicker brush, then you won't need to worry about mats anyway.

Slicker brushes are like a mixture between a pin brush and a bristle brush, but they are for a more specific purpose. A slicker brush uses pins, but they are so small they have the appearance of bristles. These are arranged into rows that part the hair as they move through it. That makes a slicker brush the best choice for dealing with matting fur. Each of the pins on a slicker brush is twisted at the end to create a very minor effect in the shape of the pin, but doing so allows them to catch onto loose fur and tug it free. This can cause the dog some minor pain, and so it is important to be careful when using a slicker brush. This factor might make you wary of purchasing and using one, but the discomfort we cause our golden retrievers isn't for no purpose. To understand, let's finish our investigation of dog brushes by looking at the undercoat brush.

The undercoat brush is going to be your best bet for removing hairs. This brush mostly waits in the closet, not getting much use. But it comes out of storage twice a year, and when it does, it is a powerful ally in the battle against shed hair. The pins on an undercoat brush are spaced far apart, and they are strong enough to deal with tough tangles in your golden retriever's undercoat. Getting rid of these knots can also cause discomfort to the puppy, and so it doesn't need to be used often. While you can run a bristle or protected pin brush through your dog's hair with some force, an undercoat brush should be used gently, and only requires one or two strokes. It will help your dog to properly shed by pulling out semi-loose fur that could otherwise get caught and cause issues. Shedding can easily lead to tangles, so it is helpful if we understand that our dog can't help shedding, and we should also take a little bit of time and effort to make the experience easier on our puppies whenever we can.

Remember, brushing is best done on a schedule. Get your dog used to being brushed daily. It is best to do general brushing after a walk so that you can remove dirt and gunk from the outdoors. But if your golden retriever has become really dirty, there is only one thing you can do.

How to Bathe a Golden Retriever

You aren't going to need to bathe your golden retriever as often as you bathe yourself, but that doesn't mean they aren't going to need washing eventually. You will, of course, need to bathe the dog if it is covered in mud or other messy substances. You'll also need to bathe your golden retriever if it is ever sprayed by a skunk. While this might be an uncommon experience, I have yet to meet a pet owner from the countryside that hasn't had a skunk story of their own to share. But while these experiences clearly require bathing, we should also get into the habit of washing our golden retrievers from time to time anyway, to keep them healthy and safe.

How often you should wash your golden retriever is going to depend on the way it lives. If we are talking about an older dog that doesn't go outside and run around very much anymore, then we will need to bathe them less often. But if we are talking about a puppy or an adult golden retriever that has been kept in shape, then we can expect more baths in our future. If you take your golden retriever out swimming a lot, then you will need to bathe them more often than a dog that sticks to running. Keep in mind that where your dog is running will also have an effect. If you are in a city that is mostly paved, you will need to wash your dog less often than one that gets to run along a dirt road that kicks up little dust storms with each stride.

Despite calculating a few easy activities that we can base our bathing off (such as giving a bath after any swimming), this doesn't actually give us a very solid idea of how often we should be doing this. One of the reasons for this is the fact that every dog is different, and how dirty yours gets is going to depend on how they behave and where they are allowed to play and run. You might think it would just be easier to bathe your golden retriever every night, but this can be harmful to the dog's fur. Those same natural oils that we want to spread through brushing can be washed off if they are bathed too often. Just as humans shouldn't use shampoo every single day, a dog is better off letting their natural oils protect them rather than rely on a bath. Bathing will also irritate a golden retriever's skin, and this can cause dandruff as skin cells become dry, die, and then fall off. So you might think you are better off not bathing your dog at all, but this can lead to foul odors and attract fleas.

Nailing down the perfect bathing schedule isn't easy, but it doesn't need to be that difficult. Start by planning to give your golden retriever a bath every month and a half so that in three months, it gets two baths. This is your baseline for an average golden retriever. Older dogs that aren't overly active won't need to be washed this often, and so you can probably roll it back to once every two months. Younger golden retrievers and especially puppies are going to be more likely to be washed earlier than this. Again, if they are caked in mud or have been swimming in natural waters, then they should be bathed right away, but make sure you adjust the schedule to reflect this. For example, if I washed my golden retriever on Monday, then I would wash her again on Thursday if she got caked in mud. While far less than a month and a half has gone by, it is more important to clean off the mud than it is to worry about the health of the coat. But I would note this extra cleaning, and then schedule the next one to be a month and a half afterward rather than the Monday one.

So we know how often we should bathe our golden retrievers, but that leaves us to explore how we manage this. We may choose to bathe them indoors using the bathtub, but a garden hose in the backyard can achieve the same results without all the mess. Regardless of where you decide to bathe your golden retriever, you are going to have pretty much the same experience. We'll walk through this to make it as painless as possible for us, but we should take a moment to remember that our dog is a living being who is involved in this experience. For us, this is a bath. For our dog, this is another game. They get to splash around, get soaked, have lots of affection and attention poured over them, and plenty of pats. For a dog, bathing is a super-fun experience, and keeping this in mind can make it more enjoyable for us owners as well.

So, keeping in mind that this is a game for your dog, you are going to need some way to reward them for properly behaving and letting you clean them fully. This can be as simple as a treat or as complicated as allowing them to play with the hose and the water after they are clean. Using fun is one way to get your golden retriever to listen, but the treat is going to be the easier way to go. When it comes to dogs, we use their stomachs in order to train them. A dog can't resist a treat, so if you teach them to expect one after a bath, then they are far more likely to behave and listen. Of course, this takes time, and multiple experiences only reinforce the behavior. The first few times you bathe your golden retriever are likely going to be a little hectic. It can be useful to get a family member or friend to help you out by looking after the dog and helping to keep them calm through petting and a soothing voice.

The first step to bathing your golden retriever is to gather everything you are going to need. If you are shampooing or conditioning your dog's fur, then grab those items, a towel or two for afterward, too. If you aren't using a hose, then you will want to grab a pot, pan, or pitcher for easy rinsing. You may purchase a bathing brush for your dog, though you don't have to. This makes it easier to work shampoo through their coat, but this can be done by hand. What you definitely don't want to skip out on is some petroleum jelly. While it may seem weird to be reaching for the petroleum jelly before a shower, it is a must-purchase item. By putting a little bit of petroleum jelly around your golden retriever's eyes, nose, and ears, you create a barrier that makes it harder for soap to get into and irritate the dog's system.

Next, give your dog a thorough brushing. You are going to want to brush them again at the end of the bath, too. In fact, if you bought a shower brush, then you'll be brushing the dog during the bath as well. Matted fur has the annoying habit of getting even more tightly tangled and hard to fix when it is wet. Brushing the golden retriever before the shower will work out these mats. Brushing during the shower is useful for getting shampoo into hard-to-reach spots, but it is also more likely to cause mats rather than work them out. What we absolutely don't want to do is skip the first brushing and then make mats worse with the second brushing. Instead, brush your dog before the shower, and then brush them as part of the aftercare to work out any mats caused during the shampooing process. This equals a lot of dog brushing time, but bathing isn't a frequent activity, and so you really might as well give it the extra couple of minutes it takes to do it thoroughly.

Brushing the dog is the simple part. The hard part is getting them to go where you want when it is time for the bath. It is best to use a tub rather than a shower, and if you are using an outdoor hose, then you should get yourself a swimming pool or metal tub that fits the dog. You want water to collect at the bottom of the tub to make the experience easier. This water will end up with lots of soap, shampoo, and conditioner in it, and this will make the mixture very clean. If your dog doesn't want to get into the tub, then you can use his stomach against him again by offering a treat. Once the dog is in the tub, it is better to use a toy to keep him there, rather than more treats. Excessive treats lead to fat dogs. Remember that you are in charge of the treats, not the dog.

You don't want to use hot water. If it is a hot day, then you will want to go with cool, almost cold water. If the weather isn't very hot, then stick with room temperature, maybe even slightly warm water. It is always best to get the water temperature set right before plugging the tub or putting the hose in it. Backyard hoses, especially black ones, absorb a great deal of heat from the sun, and this, in turn, causes sitting water to get way too hot for our dogs. Always run the water to the right temperature to avoid causing any harm or discomfort to your golden retriever.

Once you have the dog in the water, you will want to get water all over the fur. Use a pot to pour water over your dog. If you are using a hose, be mindful of how much pressure it has. You wouldn't want to put a powerful hose too close to your dog, and you never want to spray them in the face directly. It is important to fully soak a golden retriever's coat, and to remember they have a double coat; you will need to make sure you aren't just washing the outside layer. Work your hands through the dog's fur, getting down against the skin. Once it is entirely soaked, you can then move onto shampoo and conditioner.

If you have been working your hands through your dog's fur to get the coat fully wet, then you have already been making the same motions necessary to shampoo them. Squeeze some shampoo on to the dog or on your hands and start working it through the fur. You want to make sure that you are working it through all of the hair and down against the skin again. You will want to do this all over the dog. All four legs, belly, neck, back, sides, tail. Be especially mindful of where limbs connect and bend, as it is easy for dirt to hide in these crevices. After the dog is fully covered, rinse it off. Repeat this cycle with the conditioner to finish with washing.

Rinsing off the dog is easy with a hose, and it can even make for a fun game at the end of the bath. Let the dog step out of the outdoor tub and chase after the water for a bit. Hit them with it from time to time to use a combination of air drying and rinsing to clean them off. But if you are rinsing shampoo before adding conditioner, you will want to keep them in the tub. Pour water over them from above so that the shampoo washes off and into the water at the bottom. It's okay to continue rinsing the dog using this water as the shampoo will be so diluted that it functions as a soap to make the water less clingy. This process takes longer with a golden retriever than it does a shorter haired dog. The double coat makes it much easier for shampoo to find plenty of places to cling on to. Make sure that you are thorough when rinsing off your golden retriever, and go over their entire coat several times.

Drying off a golden retriever is also harder compared to less hairy dogs. Use your towel to pat the dog's coat dry. You can use the towel to pet the dog dry, following the direction of the hair itself. But avoid rubbing the dog all over like you were scratching its tummy. It is tempting to clean your animal this way, but it is healthier for their coat if you are careful of it. You should also be prepared for the dog to shake itself and spray water everywhere. There's a reason every cartoon dog in history has had to shake off a comical amount of water. They really do shake off like that, and it can get messy. You can use a towel to block most of the damage if you are loose enough to let the dog shake.

GOLDEN RETRIEVER

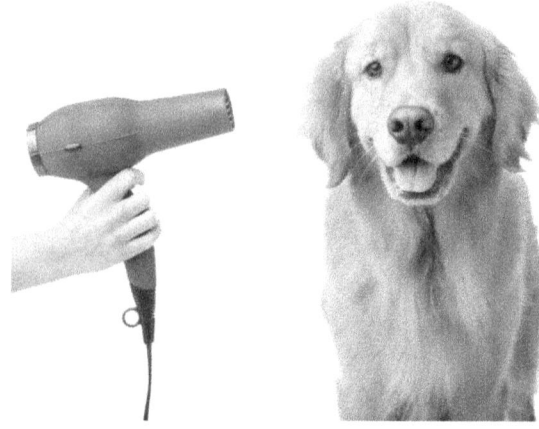

The most efficient way to get a golden retriever dry is to use a blowdryer. You need to be careful not to burn them by holding it too close, but it allows you to get in and around all the parts of the dog to dry them off. If you are worried about the damage a wet dog could cause to your household, then you are going to want to purchase a blowdryer for the colder months. Air drying outside is an option if the weather is warm. A wet dog shouldn't be put outside when it is cold; that's just mean. But if it is warm out, then you can let the dog air dry outside for a little bit. Just make sure they can't get into anything too messy, or you might find yourself having a long day, bathing your golden retriever for a second time.

Between brushing and bathing, you now have the knowledge necessary to keep your golden retriever's fur coat beautiful and clean. But that fur keeps growing, and it will eventually need to be cut. When that happens, you'll need to turn to trimming.

How to Trim a Golden Retriever

Trimming your golden retriever doesn't need to be a very tricky or time-consuming experience. If you are going to be giving the dog an entire haircut, then this might take you a while, and you are going to need to be extremely careful not to damage the dog's coat. You are still going to need to be careful, even when doing simple trimming, but full coat cuts require a level of attention and caution that comes from a trained professional. Nonetheless, you can trim up a golden retriever's coat and carefully remove any mats with a pair of scissors and a couple of minutes.

To begin with, your dog must be dry so you can see what needs to be cut. This is even more important for cutting mats, as wet mats are much tighter. Since the golden retriever has a double coat, we need to be careful and only cut one of the coats. You will mostly want to trim the overcoat, but there may be occasions when the undercoat needs a quick fix. Never cut both layers at the same time, only one or the other. While this double coat helps with trudging through water, it also works to regulate the golden retriever's temperature by trapping air between the two layers of fur. Cutting one layer is okay, but when you cut through both, you destroy this effect entirely. This is why you need to be especially careful with full coat cuts.

Start by trimming the paw and getting any long hairs that are sticking out from the bottom. Check between each of the dog's toes and be careful when trimming the hair here. Following the feet, move on to the legs. You don't ever want to cut the fur off entirely, but just give it a simple trim to get it a little bit shorter and even. If you look at your dog, you will notice that they have more fur in the back then the front. Try to keep this ratio in mind when trimming, so that the cut looks natural. This is all overcoat. Many of the following steps are for the overcoat as well, but we are going to switch to undercoat after we finish with the legs.

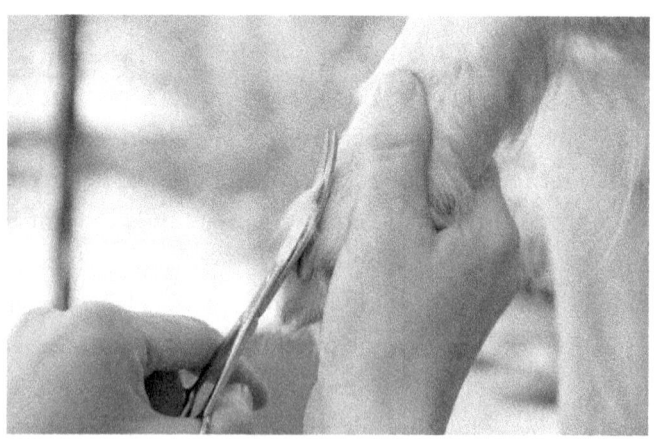

When we move onto the torso of the dog and get to the chest and neck, we trim the undercoat rather than the overcoat. You will notice there is actually much less overcoat in these areas when compared to the legs. The chest area is notorious for mats, and it always seems to grow quicker than the rest of the dog. You want to even it up and remove any mats you find. There is no proper length for this part of the dog, and so it is best to trim with cleanliness in mind. Remove anything that is tangled or getting to look really bad. The length of this section is rarely ever even, so you shouldn't need to focus on it too much.

Move onto the ears and around the face. This requires you to be very careful not to harm your dog. It can be a good idea to wait until they are sleeping before doing this part, though a distraction may be able to help as well. You only want to take a few snips off to clean up around the ear. You'll notice the dog's face doesn't have a lot of fur, but once you get to the ears, it seems like there is a forest. Trim this off carefully. Keep in mind that reducing the hair around the ears is healthy for a golden retriever, and so this doubles as illness prevention.

You don't need to trim a golden retriever's tail unless it starts to get matted, but if you want to, you should make sure you don't make it too short. Dogs can communicate a lot with their tails, and you wouldn't want to take that away from there. Other than that, you now have a freshly trimmed dog. This will leave you with a lot of dog hair to toss out. Speaking of which…

What to Do With a Shedding Golden Retriever

There are three elements for us to discuss to best deal with our golden retriever's shedding. We should discuss why dogs shed, when they shed, and what we can do about it. By doing this, you will understand why this is so vital to our doggos, and you can prepare your household to deal with it ahead of time, rather than be blindsided by a storm of furballs.

We'll start with why because it's the easiest one. Dogs shed to keep their temperature at a healthy level. Sometimes called a summer coat and winter coat, you can think of a dog as having a warm coat and a cold coat. When it is warm out, they don't need to have such a heavy coat because this would get too hot. But a thin coat won't be warm enough for the winter. There are many animals that go through shedding like this, but a golden retriever is going to shed a lot. You could build a new dog out of the amount of fur a golden retriever loses. But this is a core process for golden retrievers because they have the double coat that traps cold or warm air between the layers of fur. This has to grow in properly, or it doesn't work.

We've already pretty much covered the "when" of shedding. You can expect two shedding periods every year. As the length of the day changes during the summer spring and the fall, this will start the shedding process for your dog. Indoor dogs won't shed as much as outside dogs do since their exposure to the changing of the day length isn't going to be as strong. But even indoor dogs will lose a lot of hair and quickly make a mess when they shed. Thankfully, you will know when these periods of shedding are, and so you can plan ahead for them. But there are a few other things that trigger this process that you need to be aware of.

Puppies have an extra shedding period where they lose the fur they had when they were young. This fur coat is in the way of the adult coat the same way that our baby teeth are in the way of our adult teeth. The fully-grown coat can't grow in until the young one is gone.

GOLDEN RETRIEVER

This will typically begin by the time they are six months old. This one-time shedding can't be avoided. Also, golden retrievers will shed for a couple of months after being fixed. All of the chemicals in their system are confused and unsure of what to do, and this causes them to shed. Their bodies are basically confused and shedding for no reason, but it is important to get your pets fixed, so this is a one time trigger that you can expect to deal with.

There are health reasons that may cause your golden retriever to shed as well. Excessive licking can cause their hair to start falling out, and it is typically a sign of a deeper underlying issue. Such issues include poor diet, which can leave a golden retriever with irritated skin. It might be due to allergies that could make the dog scratch and itch to the point of losing hair. The animal might have a problem with fleas or other parasitic pests. Not only that, but the most common reason for a dog to lick or scratch excessively is stress. A stressed-out golden retriever will lick, scratch, and shed like crazy.

So, you can expect two normal sheds a year, plus a puppy shed, and a shed after they are fixed. Anything beyond this is a sign something is bothering your puppy, and you should investigate further. But even accepting just the healthy sheds, there's going to be a lot of hair to take care of. Let's tackle them before we move on to keeping our golden retrievers healthy.

It turns out, the best way to deal with shedding is to brush your golden retriever. If you've been following the advice in this chapter, then you've already learned how to deal with shedding. What's the other way you can help your golden retriever shed? Give them a bath and blow-dry them afterward. If you are brushing your dog throughout this period, then you won't have nearly as much loose hair getting all over the place. But really, with a golden retriever, you are going to want to think of ways to make household fur easier.

Furniture covers can help to keep hair off chairs and couches. When the shedding season is done, they can be removed and easily washed. You'll also want to have a vacuum cleaner because otherwise, you'd pretty much be doomed to a furry existence. A lint roller will help you to clean off clothes and other fabrics that attract hair. By brushing the dog and removing the hair, you take away most of it. Using these tools and tricks will let you clean up the rest without much effort.

GOLDEN RETRIEVER

Chapter Summary

- A golden retriever's fur hangs quite low to the ground, and this makes it notorious for getting muddy and dirty. All this mess can be dragged through your house if you aren't careful to bathe your golden retriever and look after their hygiene.

- Golden retrievers have medium-length coats, but this amounts to a whole lot of fur, as you'll discover whenever they shed.

- Coats can get dirty quickly, and they are prone to trap dirt, so it's important to brush them properly. Brushing helps to remove free dirt and grime that can cause issues if left to fester.

- Golden retrievers tend to develop lots of tangles in their fur. Mats can be hard to brush out, though a solid brushing routine will limit their frequency. Matted hair may need to be cut if you can't brush it out completely.

- Golden retrievers have a "double coat" of fur. Their coats are two layers, an inner and an outer. This allows them to trap air between the two layers to regulate their temperature. While these coats will also help them to have less issues with sickness from dirt, plus they'll dry off much easier after coming out of water, having a double coat also leads to more issues with matting.

GOLDEN RETRIEVER

- Hygiene problems with the inner coat can be hard to catch if you aren't being mindful to groom your dog. You might find them looking unhappy and smelling slightly odd, only to discover you missed an issue with the inner coat that you could quickly fix.

- Brushing your golden retriever's fur helps spread healthy oils through the coat to keep it looking beautiful and shining. It also helps you to build a bond with your golden retriever because they're going to love the grooming.

- Spending time brushing your golden retriever is a great way to get them used to having people in their space. This can make it easier to bring them to the vet later on.

- There are different brushes for different purposes. These range from pin and bristle brushes to undercoat brushes and slicker brushes. While you will only really need a pin brush or a bristle brush, you will likely want one of each type.

- Pin or bristle brushes will both work for a general-purpose brush. Pin brushes use little metal pins, and bristle brushes use thin bristles. You may want to invest in a comb with plastic-tipped pins to ensure you never hurt the dog by accident when brushing too hard.

- Slicker brushes are a mixture of pin and bristle brushes, but they are used to help break apart matted fur and clear up tangles. These brushes can cause a small amount of discomfort to a dog with a tangle, and so you should only use them from time to time, and never more than two passes at a time.

- Undercoat brushes are used to remove hairs from a dog's coat. That's great for using during the shedding season. Fur that doesn't properly come out when it is time, can lead to issues with the replacement coat growing back in properly.

- Bathing a golden retriever only needs to happen every month and a half, unless you find yourself with a muddy dog or one that was swimming around in a natural lake or river. Wash these dogs right away to prevent issues or messes.

- Remember that washing your dog will seem like a game to them, and so treats will make it easier for them to learn their part in the game.

- Dogs might not want to get into a tub at first. Two people can be useful when first teaching a golden retriever how to have a bath. One person cleans the dog while the other keeps it calm.

- Use lukewarm water and always have the water at the right temperature before you put your golden retriever in the tub.

- You may want to bathe your golden retriever outside to avoid soaking the bathroom. If you do, remember that water in a garden hose is very

GOLDEN RETRIEVER

hot at first. Don't accidentally burn your furbaby.

- Get everything you need for bathing your golden retriever in place before you get the dog in the tub. Shampoo, towels, toys, treats, a pot for scooping water, whatever you need should be gathered first.

- Start by pouring water over the dog and using your hands to work the water through all of the overcoat and down to the undercoat and the skin beneath. Once the dog is completely wet, add shampoo and continue working it in.

- Use a pot or scoop to pour water over the dog to rinse away all of the shampoo. Repeat these steps with the conditioner if you have any.

- Putting a little bit of petroleum jelly around your golden retriever's nose, eyes, and ears can prevent water and soap from getting in and causing irritation and discomfort.

- You should always brush your dog before you bathe it, as water will make mats even tighter and harder to get loose.

- Drying off a golden retriever can take a long time, but it is made easier by allowing the dog to have a good shake. Hold a towel around the dog, so water doesn't go everywhere. You may also want to use a blowdryer to make this quicker.

GOLDEN RETRIEVER

- When trimming a golden retriever, it is vital to only cut either the outer layer or the inner layer at a time. When we work on the legs, the tail, the neck, and the ears, we are cutting the outer layer. We cut the inner layer when working on the chest area. While this switches between outer and inner, it should never be both in the same location. If that happened, it would ruin your golden retriever's ability to regulate its temperature.

- Golden retrievers shed twice a year. They shed in the fall to lose their summer coat and grow in their winter one. Then in the spring, they start to lose the winter coat in place of the latest summer fashion.

- Golden retrievers will need to shed their puppy fur when they are growing up. Getting fixed also causes a few months of shedding, while the chemicals and hormones in the dog learn to rebalance themselves.

- Dogs might start to shed for health reasons, so keep an eye out for off-season shedding as it can be an early warning sign.

- The best way to deal with a shedding golden retriever is to brush them often with an undercoat brush. You'll want lint brushes to pick dog hair off clothes, and it isn't a bad idea to cover the furniture with sheets to make post-shedding cleanup easier on yourself.

In the next chapter, you will learn all about how to keep your golden retriever in the best health possible. We'll take a look at their life expectancy, what warning signs can let us know if we are dealing with infections or allergies, and what hereditary diseases they may have. We shall examine how exercise and diet work together to keep your golden retriever strong, fit, happy, and healthy.

CHAPTER FIVE

KEEPING YOUR GOLDEN RETRIEVER HEALTHY

In the last chapter, we saw how to keep our golden retriever looking beautiful. In this chapter, we learn how to keep them healthy so that they can experience a wonderful life filled with happiness, love, and joy. Of course, a sick golden retriever isn't going to feel very well, but that won't stop them from sharing their love with you and your family. But the discomfort that sickness brings your dog will leave them with less energy, and they'll be far more stressed-out than they should be. Worst yet, it is heartbreaking when a member of the family is sick. It doesn't matter if they're your child, your lover, or they're covered in fur.

We'll start this chapter by looking at the lifespan of a golden retriever. This will give us a basis for understanding what point of their lifecycle they're in. Just as we humans get weaker as we get older, so do our golden retrievers. But getting weaker doesn't necessarily mean getting unhealthy, thankfully. From there, we'll move into looking at common ailments that golden retrievers are susceptible to, and we'll follow this with a discussion on the hereditary diseases that, unfortunately, curse these delightful canines. With all these negatives stacking up, we'll switch gears, and finish with some positives by learning healthy exercises and dieting advice that will keep your golden retriever in the best possible shape.

The Lifespan of a Golden Retriever

Perhaps this is the saddest part of the book, and it breaks my heart to write it. A few decades ago, the lifespan of a golden retriever was between fifteen to eighteen years. If your parents adopted a golden retriever when you were born, then the dog would still be around to celebrate your sweet sixteenth with you, or even your first time voting. But recently, the lifespan of golden retrievers has become much shorter, and now they are only expected to live a dozen years. Often less rather than more.

This change in lifespan is still not fully understood by science, though studies have been conducted in order to figure out this troubling statistic. As best as we can tell right now, the cause is due to many factors working together. It could be all of these causes, or it could be a single one of them, but there are too many in play to say exactly what is causing it yet. We can take a quick moment to consider some of these factors to get a better picture.

Cancer is a big killer of golden retrievers. In fact, compared to any other type of dog out there, golden retrievers are most likely to die from cancer. This is another fact that scientists are still trying to understand, but there has yet to be any clear evidence as to why this is. Not only does cancer kill golden retrievers the most, but it also doesn't just wait for old age. Even golden retrievers less than a year old can develop cancer. Dogs that passed away early due to cancer are one factor that keeps the lifespan expectancy down. This is horrible, but the silver lining is that young cases bring the whole number down, and therefore healthy dogs have a better chance at living longer than the average. Scientists are looking into possible environmental factors that may be causing cancer in these wonderful dogs, and so, hopefully, a solution to this troubling issue will be found soon.

While scientists look towards environmental factors, we will be turning our attention towards hereditary diseases in a few moments. It deserves mentioning here that golden retrievers have serious hip problems. While these aren't life-threatening, they will reduce the overall quality of a golden retriever's life. Pain in the hip can lead to less exercise and movement, which in turn leads to a weakened immune system and possibly obesity (itself a factor in exacerbating health issues). While the oldest golden retriever to have ever lived made it to twenty years, this would never have been possible without proper diet and exercise. The risk of developing hip problems is high in golden retrievers, but sound exercise and diet will keep the risk as low as possible so that your golden retriever can stay healthy and fit enough for a dozen or more years in your family.

Common Ailments Golden Retrievers Face

Golden retrievers are sweet and affectionate dogs, but they are also prone to a lot of health issues. We've talked briefly about cancer already. Cancer could go on this list as well, but we'll be fundamentally talking about eyes and hips when we discuss hereditary diseases. Technically speaking, cancer isn't inherited, but the golden retriever has certainly developed a definite vulnerability to this horrible disease. For now, let's focus on allergies, ear infections, skin conditions, and the other common ailments which we can keep an eye out for.

Skin Conditions:

Skin conditions are among the most common issues that golden retrievers have to deal with. That double coat of theirs that helps to keep them cool, is also likely to trap germs and pathogens that promote skin problems.

GOLDEN RETRIEVER

Skin conditions may be easy to confuse with allergies because both lead to scratching and flaking, and raw skin results from this. Skin conditions cause problems with the skin *before* the scratching, allergies cause skin issues *because* of the scratching. Problems with your golden retriever's skin may be the result of mold, pests like fleas, or simple dirt that has been trapped too long. Common issues include lick granuloma, which is caused when a dog spends too much time licking its legs; lipomas, which are benign tumors that form in the fatty tissue beneath the skin; seborrhea, which is a chronic disease that causes the sebaceous glands to release too much oil in their coats, or sebaceous cysts, which form in the sebaceous gland. Another common issue is sebaceous adenitis, but this is a hereditary disease that we'll be looking at in a moment. If your golden retriever is showing signs of a skin condition, then take them into the vet. There are many treatments available that can relieve your dog's pain and discomfort.

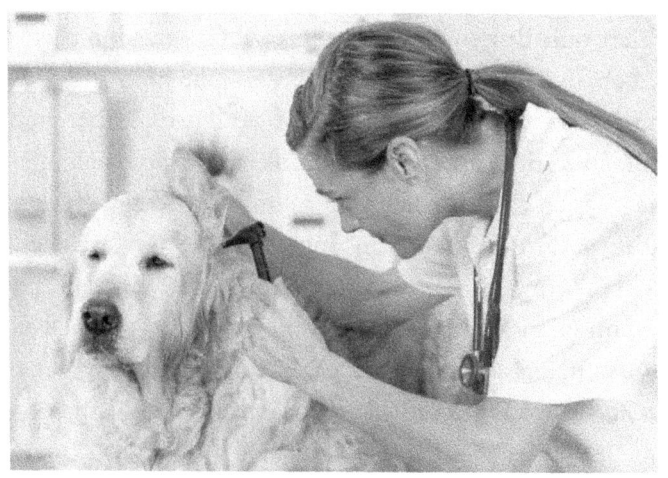

Ear Infections:

Ear infections in dogs are easy to treat. This is great news because ear infections are one of the most uncomfortable experiences that any species can go through. Ear infections aren't unique to golden retrievers; they are a common ailment for dogs of every breed. However, the golden retriever does have large ears, and they tend to flop around when they run, and dangle down when they rest. This does two things. The first thing it does is make it easy for dirt, dust, and gunk to get into a golden retriever's ears while they are exercising or playing. It does the second thing while they rest. Since a golden retriever's ears hang down, there isn't much room for air to flow through them. In dogs that have upright ears, the air is a great ally that helps to clean them out. But since golden retriever's ears don't let in much air, dirt and germs are able to take hold and grow into infections much easier. If you notice that your golden retriever is scratching at its ear a lot or shaking its head, then this can be a sign of an ear infection. Take a look and see if you can spot any crusting, swelling, redness, or discharge coming from the ear. Also, pay attention to your nose as an infected ear will smell far worse than a healthy ear does. Ear infections are easy to treat, but you will still want to catch it early so that it is quicker to fix.

Allergies:

Dogs get allergies just like us humans do. Pretty much any biological creature can develop allergies. Trying to figure out if your dog has allergies isn't easy to do since many of the symptoms of allergies also point towards other common issues like skin ailments. Unfortunately, golden retrievers have a tendency to get allergies more than most breeds, and so the chances are high that yours will too at some point. Again, it can be hard to tell if your dog has an allergy because the most common warning sign is excessive scratching. If you notice that your dog is scratching more than usual, then you will want to keep an eye on it and consider taking it to the vet soon. Other symptoms of allergies range from runny eyes to diarrhea, vomiting, sneezing, and even snoring. While vomiting, diarrhea, and sneezing are all easy to identify, it isn't so easy to link snoring to an ailment, but it just might be the result of an itchy, swollen throat due to allergies.

Dogs can develop allergies to pretty much anything from pollen to shampoo, cigarette smoke, and dust mites. If it can cause an allergic reaction in a human, then it might also be able to produce one in your golden retriever. The best thing to do if you suspect allergies is to take them to the vet and get a professional opinion. There might be issues in the diet that could be to blame, but if the vet also suspects allergies, then they can order some tests to make sure. The most common way to check for allergies is through a blood test. This can cause dogs to get worked up, and so they're usually sedated prior to the test. Your dog isn't in any harm from this, but they are going to be confused and a little drug-addled when they wake up, so be prepared to be attentive to their needs as they come back around.

If you suspect allergies, then you may want to first start by cleaning up the living space. You might find some mold or rotted food that could be causing an issue, and that's allowing dangerous pathogens to get into the living space. Make sure to get in between cracks and under tables and chairs to clear away all the dust. That might do the trick. If not, then you could try removing possible triggers one at a time to see if the dog's condition improves. This method can be a cheap way to figure out what is causing the allergies. You should also try changing any shampoo, soap, conditioner, or other products that you use to clean your golden retriever. Just make sure that you don't change these at the same time you are removing a possible trigger from the living space; otherwise, you won't be able to determine which factor was the issue without further testing and possible doggy discomfort.

Food allergies are also very common in golden retrievers, and so owners often discover that a change in diet can make all the difference in the world. We can test for food allergies by changing what we feed our dogs, but again, we need to do this at a separate time from grooming or environment trigger testing. If you suspect food might be the cause, then begin by switching their primary source of protein. If they are eating chicken products, you could change this for fish or cow products. You should also switch their treats, but this should be done separately. You may remove treats from the diet while altering their protein, but you are better off leaving them in to ensure that the change was from the protein, and not the treats themselves. If you take your golden retriever to the vet, then you should ask them about healthy diets.

There isn't a whole lot that we can do for our dogs when they have allergies. It takes time to test for what the triggers are, and while this is happening, our dogs are going to be uncomfortable. We may be unable to prevent our dogs from getting allergies, but, thankfully, there are hundreds of brands of medications on the market from creams to pills or even shots that can allow your dog to continue living its life in relative comfort until the trigger is discovered and removed.

Hereditary Diseases in Golden Retrievers

It is common for golden retrievers to be afflicted with some form of hereditary disease. While you can reduce the likelihood by purchasing a puppy from a healthy mother, there are plenty of hereditary diseases that are known for skipping a generation or two only to come back in full force twenty years down the bloodline. In general, golden retrievers are dogs that have to deal with a lot of medical issues, and inherited problems aren't any different in that respect.

Hip Dysplasia:

We've briefly touched on hip dysplasia already, but it is a hereditary issue that can cripple a golden retriever if it isn't looked after. Hip dysplasia is a term used to describe a growth in the hip joint; it's essentially a form of arthritis. If you have ever played with an action figure or a doll, then you have seen first-hand how the joints of our bodies are round balls that fit into specific spots on the body. When everything is healthy, the bones fit together tightly in the joint, and the round shape allows them to move in all directions. When hip dysplasia develops, the fit between ball and nook isn't right anymore. That results in pain and a limited range of movement. This can be due to an issue with the ball growing too large or misshapen, or it can be an issue where the socket isn't the right size.

Hip dysplasia can stop your golden retriever from wanting to exercise, and this weakens its system in general. Unfortunately, the only way to treat the condition is to seek medical treatment. If you don't, then the issue can get much worse and immobilize your pet. But proper exercise and weight control will help to reduce the development of hip dysplasia. You should keep in mind that your dog will need more help from you as it gets older. The joints in its body are going to get weaker naturally. Using a medication that reduces inflammation in the joints can help keep your dog comfortable enough to continue exercising and taking care of its health. It won't fix hip dysplasia, but it can help you to minimize the pain your dog feels as it ages or goes through treatment.

Cancer:

Golden retrievers deal with cancer more than any other breed. The Golden Retriever Club has estimated that 60% of golden retrievers will pass away due to some form of cancer. Among the most common are lymphosarcoma, osteosarcoma, and mastocytoma. The rates of cancer are about 10% higher in male dogs compared to females. Not that this does a whole lot to help out the breed: they still get cancer with rates twice as high as dogs typically do.

Identifying cancer isn't easy. Since it happens under the surface, you are most likely going to try to attribute an environmental cause to your dog's sluggishness. One big problem with cancer is that it weakens the dog's immune system so that it is more susceptible to other ailments. Not only does this result in a sicker dog, but it can also help to mask the underlying cancer that is at the root of the easier to identify ailments. If you suspect cancer, or are unsure why your dog seems weaker than normal, then you should bring them in to see a vet.

Cancer can be caught early and removed. This doesn't mean that your golden retriever is going to get better, unfortunately, but it does mean that they might be able to. Recovering from cancer treatment is a rough experience for a dog. They are weaker than normal and often have to wear a cone to allow time for their stitches to heal. Remember that your dog isn't going to understand what it went through, and it is going to be confused for some time until it starts to recover, and life begins to go back to normal. You will need to be there to support your golden retriever with your love and attention.

GOLDEN RETRIEVER

Von Willebrand Disease:

Von Willebrand's disease is a member of the family of diseases known as bleeding disorders. Despite the name, these diseases don't actually cause bleeding! Instead, they affect the way that blood undergoes the coagulation process in which it clots and changes from a liquid substance to a solid. When you or your golden retriever gets cut, liquid blood immediately starts to come out. But this quickly slows down due to the clotting process. Your blood coagulates around the wound to prevent further loss. Bleeding disorders like Von Willebrand disease affect the way blood coagulates, and it is, unfortunately, the most frequent bleeding disorder in both people and golden retrievers.

What Von Willebrand disease does is make it so the blood can't clot together as it should, due to a problem with the protein necessary for the function to work. Since it is a bleeding disorder, you may never see any obvious signs that your golden retriever has it. There is a very real chance that you could live out a long life with a golden retriever that had Von Willebrand disease but never showed any signs. But other golden retrievers may start to bleed from their nose, mouth, or genitals. One of the typical ways that Von Willebrand disease is found is through surgery. A dog is operated on, and the medical staff finds that the animal continues to bleed far longer than it should. Medical staff are equipped to deal with this, and so it is a common experience for a dog owner to be told that their dog has been successfully operated on for cancer, but they also have Von Willebrand disease. It should be noted that while some dogs may live their whole lives without issue, a bleeding dog should never be left untreated. Too much blood loss can lead to death.

If you think that your dog has Von Willebrand disease, then you should take them to the vet and share your concern. If the vet believes this may be the case, then they will order tests. The method used to screen for Von Willebrand disease is called a buccal mucosal bleeding time test. The vet will carefully make a tiny cut in the soft layer of the dog's nose to determine how long it bleeds. For some dogs, it is immediately clear they aren't bleeding properly. But, more often than not, what happens will either be a regular blood flow that stops when it normally should, or a regular blood flow which becomes irregular due to the length of time it goes on. If this screening test causes the veterinarian any concerns, then they will order a blood sample to be taken so that they can test for how much of the disease is present.

Most of the time, a dog with Von Willebrand disease can live a perfectly healthy and normal life. You are going to need to be careful about keeping them from getting seriously harmed, but this isn't much different from the ordinary experience of owning a dog. There are two big issues that you need to prepare for, though. The first is excess bleeding following any form of medical treatment or injections and the like. By knowing this, you can be cautious about the dog's recovery and mindful to keep a watchful eye for bleeding. This is especially important because the second issue is that you may find yourself facing excess bleeding at any time. Anytime that you find your dog bleeding, you need to watch it and make sure that it stops before it loses too much. You should know the phone number of any pet hospitals in the area because you may need to find a blood transfusion for your dog on short notice in case of an emergency. These symptoms are more likely to be caused by injury rather than naturally, but it is possible for the problem to start occurring without a clear trigger.

Sebaceous Adenitis:

The sebaceous gland is what produces the healthy oils that help to keep your golden retriever's fur beautiful and shiny. These oils are super-important for the health of the dog's skin as well as the fur. The oil basically covers the surface of the fur and the skin, and creates a layer of protection against harmful invaders. Sebaceous adenitis is an inflammation that happens inside this gland. This inflammation will start out as painful, but in time it can pretty much ruin the sebaceous glands from the inside out.

Unfortunately, sebaceous adenitis is another of those diseases which we don't understand enough about to pinpoint a cause. We do know that there are certain breeds that develop them more often than others, and this has led scientists to see it as an inherited sickness. Golden retrievers are among the list of breeds that suffer from this affliction. It is important to keep a watchful eye for signs of sebaceous adenitis so that you can treat it before it ruins the glands. There is hope of saving the glands if you catch it early enough.

You should be keeping an eye out for sebaceous adenitis whenever you are petting or grooming your dog. For golden retrievers, look out for patches of fur stuck together and patches of dandruff. Dandruff is just the shedding of dead skin cells, and it is natural for most animals to shed some dandruff. But, if you find patches of it stuck on the dog, then this is a bad sign because it means that a whole lot of skin is dying at once in that area. You may also notice that the fur around these areas begins to look dried out, and even take on slight discoloration. These signs are scary, but the good news is this disease starts around the head, so it is the part of the dog you will be petting and scratching most. If you know what to look out for, it will make it easy to spot it early and treat it before it is a problem.

Treatment itself can come in several forms. The vet is going to need to order a biopsy in order to determine how far along the disease is and what is happening inside the dog's sebaceous glands. The goal is to catch it while inflammation is still causing damage. The first thing that needs to be done before anything else, is to stop the inflammation process in its tracks. Sebaceous adenitis damages the dog's coat, and so treatment often includes steps to promote healthy new fur to grow in. It should be noted that it is possible to fix glands that have been destroyed through this disease, but successful regeneration isn't guaranteed. We should strive to catch sebaceous adenitis early for the sake of our golden retrievers.

Treatment for this disease will include supplements of omega 3 fatty acids, as well as oil-based creams and baths that will need to be applied directly to the damaged area. Both of these will help the dog's coat to regrow. While the coat is being cared for, the disease itself is most often fought with oral applications of cyclosporine. That helps stop the inflammation process, and this is primarily what it is used for. A side effect of this is that cyclosporine may also help to encourage regeneration of damaged glands. There are alternative treatments which are starting to get more popular, but, ultimately, what the multitude of treatment approaches show us is that sebaceous adenitis is absolutely manageable if you seek treatment quickly.

Cataracts and Other Eye Problems:

Cataracts get a special mention here since they are the most frequently experienced problem when it comes to a golden retriever's eyes. Cataracts don't usually start showing up until your dog is around five years old, give or take a year. You might even notice cataracts forming on the dog's eyes as they start to take on a foggy appearance that worsens as they develop. Vision is a phenomenon when light passes through the eyeball and is understood by the brain. As cataracts get worse, less and less light is able to get into the dog's eye. So what starts out as a little bit of visual information being lost, turns into all information being lost as the dog goes blind. Cataracts are most commonly caused due to hereditary disease, but they may form naturally in old age or be caused by exposure to electricity or chemicals. They are primarily treated through surgery unless they are the result of another treatable condition.

GOLDEN RETRIEVER

Another disease that golden retrievers get a lot is central progressive retinal atrophy. CPRA is almost exclusively found in older dogs. Affecting both the eyes, the retinas are slowly wasting away, and so your golden retriever begins to have a hard time seeing things that aren't moving. CPRA is not yet treatable, and so it will be up to you to keep the home comfortable for the dog. The best way to do this is to keep the layout of your home (or at least the dog's space within it) the same so that the dog feels safe amid familiar territory. CPRA can be identified by the presence of cataracts or a greenish tint to the surface of the dog's eyeball. If you see cataracts at any point, you should get your dog into the vet anyway. You may also be able to tell that something is wrong if your dog suddenly seems scared to go exploring new places, tackle staircases, or go out into the dark. This behavior tells us that something is not right, and we should take a closer look at their eyes. They might also be clumsier than usual. If you see them getting into accidents or knocking things over, then you should take them to a vet as well.

There are lots of other problems that may start in and around the eyes. In general, you should take a good look at your dog's eyes on a regular schedule. This can be as easy as taking a glance while petting them in the morning. Look for any discoloration of the eye. It may look cloudy or milky. It could have a greenish tint or even be bloodshot. You may also notice leakage around the eyes or excessive crusting. All of these are signs that you need to take your dog into the vet and get them looked at. When it comes to the health of your pet, you should always err on the side of caution, and react quickly. While unlikely with eye issues, a single day can sometimes be the difference between life and death when it comes to treating a pet's ailments and diseases. They can't ask their owners for help, so it is up to us to be responsible for them.

Exercising a Golden Retriever

Just as all humans need exercise, all dogs need exercise. Exercise is necessary to keep living and moving organisms healthy and strong. Golden retrievers, in particular, love getting lots of exercise. Remember that they were bred to hunt waterfowl. That means trudging through water and chasing after prey and lots of training. From the dawn of their existence, they have been energetic dogs, and this hasn't changed just because they aren't hunting anymore. Golden retrievers that don't get enough exercise are more prone to cancer, hip dysplasia, and a lot of diseases and ailments that we would never wish on our furry friends.

You are going to need to give your golden retriever lots of exercise, but this doesn't mean that it has to be a tough experience for you. There are a lot of ways to help your golden retriever get a workout, and with many of them, you only have to push yourself as hard as you want to. If you are feeling especially energetic, then your dog isn't going to complain, but so long as you can provide them with a way for them to get exercise, then they are going to be perfectly happy. Some of these methods are ways you can do without moving at all if you really get creative with them.

The most common way people exercise their dogs is to take them for a walk. With a golden retriever, you are going to want to walk with them for at least an hour. Many people will give them a quick lap of the neighborhood, but this simply isn't enough exercise. If you want to invest more of yourself into your dog's exercise routine, then you should jog rather than walk. A shorter distance can provide a better workout this way, but it will require more of you. If you can only manage a walk, then you should combine it with one of the other exercises we're looking at. Keep in mind that this doesn't apply to hiking. If you are going over rough terrain or hitting a trail for an extended length of time, then your golden retriever is going to love it and get a fantastic workout.

If you can't jog with your dog, then why not take them out to the nearest dog park and play fetch? If you have a backyard that is large enough, you might not even have to leave your own property for this. Fetch is particularly great for golden retrievers because it takes them back to their hunting roots. Grab a tennis ball or a frisbee and give it a toss. In a second, your dog is going to be off like a rocket. Excited dogs often bring the ball back but have a hard time giving it up. This is a playful behavior that lets you know your dog is having a great time. Either toss another ball or give them a moment. Even the most ball-craving dog will want to chase after it again before long. The best part of an exercise like fetch is you can sit in one place and let the dog do the work. It gets an amazing workout, and you don't have to do anything. But if you want to get more involved, then you can try racing the dog or playing keep away.

Another great exercise is playing a game of tug of war with your golden retriever. This one has a tendency to be combined with fetch in a natural way thanks to ball-hungry retrievers. But you can play tug of war indoors. Purchase a knotted rope toy or make one yourself (being careful only to use a rope that won't harm the dog's mouth). Wave the toy in front of the dog until it bites on it, and then use the other end to see which of you is the strongest. The dog will put its weight into it and work a lot of its muscles. You will also find yourself working the muscles in your arm pretty hard, so while it doesn't require a lot of movement, it can be quite exhausting. There's no shame losing to your golden retriever if you get tired. If you want another indoor activity, then try getting a laser pointer. While they are most commonly associated with cats, lots of dogs get just as much enjoyment trying to catch that elusive red dot. Just remember that they are going to go running after it, and a dog is a lot heavier than a cat, so be mindful of giving them enough space to slow down before they whack into walls or furniture.

Other activities that are good fits for golden retrievers are hunting, swimming, running, and jumping. While running can be done outdoors, you may also think about getting a treadmill to give your golden retriever an indoor sprint. Hunting is embedded in a golden retriever's blood, and it is a fantastic exercise, but clearly not an option for many people. Swimming is marvelous and can be done at indoor pet pools or lakes, rivers, and beaches. You'll want to give your golden retriever a quick bath after swimming, though indoor pet pools will have facilities for washing and drying your dog after swimming. Jumping is an easy trick you can teach your golden retriever, plus it is a great way for them to burn off a lot of calories and work the muscles throughout their hindquarters. Just make sure that there is enough space in the area before you tell them to jump; otherwise, any accidents will be your fault and not theirs. You should also take this outdoors if you have neighbors living beneath you because 65 pounds of dog makes a lot of noise when it hits the floor.

These are some of the best ways that you can exercise a golden retriever, but they are far from the only. A little imagination, and you can find thousands of other ways to inject more physical movement into your dog's life. With a golden retriever, they will pretty much be ready for anything, and more exercise is rarely a bad thing.

GOLDEN RETRIEVER

Feeding a Golden Retriever Properly

When it comes to dog food brands, you could ask a thousand different owners and get a hundred different answers for which is the best. There is such a wide variety that it becomes almost useless to try to argue which is the best. This is doubly true when brands could disappear, and new ones could pop up at any moment. Instead, we'll focus on the nutrition needs of our golden retrievers and ensure that we can provide them with that. Once you know how much your golden retriever needs to be healthy, you can then experiment with different brands to find one that fits your price range, provides plenty of nutrition, and is tasty enough to keep your golden retriever coming back for more.

GOLDEN RETRIEVER

We know that golden retrievers are quite heavy dogs with an average weight of around 65 pounds. This number is then used to figure out how many calories a healthy golden retriever should be eating in a day. The recommendation for golden retrievers that are getting lots of good exercise is between 1,353 and 1,740 calories every day. If your golden retriever isn't very active, then this number could be as low as 1,000 calories a day. As a golden retriever gets older, it isn't uncommon for them to start needing less food. Joint pain and other issues reduce how much exercise these dogs get, and this, in turn, means less food is required to keep them healthy. If your dog is on the heavy side, you will want to feed it a bit less. If it is on the light side, then you may want to try feeding it more. If you feed a light dog more, but it doesn't put on any weight, then take it in to see the vet.

If you are in North America, then any dog food that has a stamp to approve it as "complete and balanced" is a great choice. In order to get this stamp, the dog food in question needs to pass testing put in place to ensure that it really is packed with enough nutrients for a healthy dog. It is good to have dry kibble in a diet, as the roughness of it will help to keep your dog's teeth clean. On the other hand, canned food is soft and moist, and it can help a meal to go down smoothly. When feeding your golden retriever, you should put a little bit of canned food at the bottom of their bowl and then put dry food on top. The smell of the canned food will make the dog eager to eat up the bowl, and it is more likely to eat all of its dry food rather than leave the meal for long periods. Feed your golden retriever like you would a family member, and make sure they have breakfast and supper. It is better for the dog to eat its meal at once, rather than constantly making sure there is food in its dish. Serving a meal will create a feeding schedule and avoid problems with being overweight.

You can check what is in your dog's food by reading the labels, and you should always do this ahead of time. Some cheaper foods will use ash as a filler in dry food, and this has been known to cause issues in a small number of pets. This is more of a problem with cats than dogs, but you should keep an eye out anyway. Most dog food uses meat for the primary protein, but this can come from chicken, cows, fish, lamb, or other assorted animals. There will also be some healthy grains and vegetable products for fiber, plus fats, oil, and sources of vitamins and other minerals. You probably won't ever need to know most of the stuff on the label, but you should at least take note of the animal it is made from, the main grains it uses, and any other vegetable or animal products. You may discover that one of these causes allergies for your dog, and, if so, you'll need to change its diet. Knowing what it is eating will make this a lot easier to do.

If you are feeding your dog within healthy calorie ranges for its level of activity, then you shouldn't see any major changes in weight once it has reached full health.

Of course, a puppy is going to get heavier and heavier, and this weight gain is to be expected. But any other major shifts after adulthood are a sign of something wrong with your golden retriever, and you should ask for a professional medical opinion. Health should never be a secondary priority when it comes to your dog; whether it is problems with infections, disease, allergies, or weight, it pays to act early and seek help.

GOLDEN RETRIEVER

Chapter Summary

- Golden retrievers have more health problems than most breeds. This is a shame considering how much love they have to share.

- Golden retrievers used to live for fifteen to eighteen years, but recently their life expectancy has dropped down to ten to twelve years.

- Scientists aren't sure why golden retrievers are living so much shorter these days. Research is being conducted to try to get more information about this troubling fact.

- Golden retrievers get cancer more than twice as regularly as any other type of dog. This greatly reduces their expected lifespan. Puppies under a year may develop cancer, so age has nothing to do with it.

- There are a lot of common ailments that affect golden retrievers, but this is the case with many species. Golden retrievers might have higher odds of specific health issues, but they need to worry about the same health problems that other dogs do.

- Skin conditions are common with golden retrievers. Things like lick granuloma or seborrhea are issues that can reduce a golden retriever's comfort.

- Ear infections are common in golden retrievers due to the way that their ears hang and flop down. Things can easily get into a golden retriever's ear when they are running, and then get trapped there as the ear flops over the hole while they sleep.

- Dogs can develop allergies to environmental triggers like dust or pollen, as well as to food or grooming products. You can get a vet to test your dog for allergies. You can check for allergies yourself by slowly removing triggers from the dog's life, one at a time. If you remove one and see a difference, then you may have identified the problem.

- Since dogs can also be allergic to food, you may need to change what they are eating. Remembering that removing a trigger at the same time that you change their food is going to confuse your data. You won't be able to tell if the food or the trigger was the issue without further testing. Always test one change at a time.

- Golden retrievers have many inherited illnesses that trouble them. These range from hip dysplasia that can make movement painful, to cancer, Von Willebrand disease, and sebaceous adenitis. Each of these will cause your dog pain, and most of them can cause death if they aren't treated medically.

- Eye problems like cataracts are both hereditary and can develop with age. Look for a cloudy

GOLDEN RETRIEVER

appearance to your golden retriever's eyes and seek medical help to prevent blindness.

- Golden retrievers need lots of exercise. It isn't enough to take them for a walk. They need to go for jogs or power walks, they need to play fetch, or perhaps chase after laser pointers. It is important to exercise a golden retriever vigorously if you want to help them stay healthy and strong.

- Golden retrievers need to have between 1,353 and 1,740 calories every day when they are active. They only need around 1,000 to 1,200 calories if they aren't very active, but your golden retriever should be kept active to stay healthy.

- Look for a "complete and balanced" stamp on your dog's food. This is a sign of quality.

- Combine wet food with dry food to make your golden retriever's dinner more appealing to them.

- Check the label of the food you are purchasing. Look for the type of meat that it uses the most. Also, take note of any other animal products it uses. Avoid purchasing foods that use ash as a filler. Ash is more common in cat food as a filler ingredient, but it has been known to make many pets sick when eaten in large quantities.

In the next chapter, you will learn how to train your golden retriever. We'll start by looking at how well golden retrievers take to learning commands (spoilers: They're one of the most obedient of all breeds), and we'll even explore how to teach them the basic commands like sit, paw, stay, and speak. Then we'll discuss clicker training to see if it is right for you and your golden retriever.

CHAPTER SIX

TRAINING YOUR GOLDEN RETRIEVER

Getting a golden retriever is always a good choice if you want a breed that follows commands and aims to please. But in order for them to follow commands, they need to be taught them. This will take a little bit of time and effort on your part, plus some patience. Golden retrievers tend to be quick learners when it comes to training, but young puppies may get confused and not catch on right away. Try to give your puppy patience and understanding. When you do, you'll find they pick up things quicker than you expected. Puppies always seem to grow up before you even have time to realize it.

In this chapter, we'll spend a few moments looking at the distinctive qualities of golden retrievers that make them one of the best-trained breeds around. From that, we'll look at basic training technique, and what basic commands all golden retrievers should learn. We'll look at a few fun commands as well, just to add a little life into our training. Finally, we'll also take a moment to discuss clicker training. This technique has become popular in the last few years as technology has made it easier than ever. It might just be the perfect approach for your training routine.

What's So Special About Training a Golden Retriever?

Golden retrievers aren't merely hunting dogs, although they did start that way. But in modern times, they might also be involved in helping law enforcement agents sniff out drugs or weapons. They can help in tracking game, or be brilliant for search and rescue. They are also used in therapy, and in assisting people with disabilities throughout their daily existence. Plus, golden retrievers are used in sports and competitions as well. The reason that golden retrievers can do all of these jobs is partly due to the fact that they are intelligent animals that love being around and pleasing humans. But they have another trait which makes them perfect for training.

Golden retrievers are very patient dogs. Of course, younger dogs are more likely to be hyper and playful. But overall, as a breed, golden retrievers are simple to train thanks to their patient natures. They will listen to you, watch your movements, and respond when you prompt them to. They're also loving beasts, so they don't get frustrated with training the way that some other breeds do. Training a golden retriever is basically about teaching them what the proper response to a prompt is. If you tell them to sit, then the right reaction is to sit. Once a golden retriever has realized this, then it is easy to reinforce the teaching and make it last a lifetime.

Golden retrievers listen best when they are being trained by their owner, as this is the person they usually have the closest bond with. When training, owners need to speak loudly, clearly, and with authority. Golden retrievers are drawn to people that demonstrate qualities of leadership. While the concept of "alpha wolves" has been debunked in recent years, golden retrievers are drawn towards humans that demonstrate some of these alpha traits. What this means for the owner is simply to treat the dog like you would a child. Be kind but firm, and make it clear that you are in command. This should, of course, never manifest itself in abuse or physical punishments. Instead, learning how to vocalize a powerful "No" will be more than enough to command respect.

When it comes to training dogs in general, it is better to start when they are young. The sooner you can begin your lessons, the more likely good behavior patterns will form. Commands learned earlier in life are also stronger and more likely to be remembered even by elderly dogs with memory problems. Essentially, the neural pathways that make up the command are firmer and harder to break when developed earlier in life. Training should also be an ongoing process. You should only focus on training a single skill at a time, moving on to more skills once the fundamentals have been mastered. These training sessions should be daily, but you don't need more than 20 minutes at a time. By keeping them short and focused, it will be more fun for your golden retriever and easier for them to figure out what you are trying to teach them.

Training a Golden Retriever

GOLDEN RETRIEVER

The best way to train a golden retriever is to follow the old fashioned approach. This is a simple process wherein you train the puppy by rewarding it when it achieves the goal. In turn, you need to refrain from rewarding behavior that is antithetical to your purpose. If you are trying to teach something like sit, then you would reward the puppy after it sits and only then. If you were trying to train it to keep off the couch, then you need to prevent this negative behavior; make sure you don't get tricked into rewarding it when it tugs on your emotions by giving you those big ol' eyes. If you stick to this basic reward/no reward system, then you can pretty much teach your golden retriever to do nearly anything.

Good rewards for this method include food or play, but food is definitely the more effective one! In fact, using food to train behavior is so effective that scientists have found it is as effective for us humans as it is for our pets. Treats impact directly on the body with sugars and salts and other elements that it craves. So, when we give a dog a treat, we are providing a biological and chemical incentive to repeat the behavior that leads to the reward.

It is a good idea to take a few minutes before you adopt a golden retriever and think about what skills you want it to know. Sit, stay, come, and lay down are all musts. But you may also want to teach them skills for exercising such as fetch or jump. Skills like roll over, play dead, or shake are all neat and fun to teach, but they don't serve a practical purpose. When you plan out what you want to teach, you can start to see connections between the skills, and it becomes easy to see how learning a skill like sit would make it easier to learn how to shake paws. You should make sure you start with the fundamentals since these are going to be used the most. Bear in mind also, that only one skill should be concentrated on at a time.

Speaking of commands, let's consider a few of the basics, and take a quick peek at what cool and weird skills we might want to teach our golden retrievers simply because it's fun!

Commands for Your Golden Retriever

When it comes to commands, we can teach as many as we want. But, for many owners, there is simply no reason to teach their dogs a bunch of tricks. They simply want their dog to do what the owner wants and, thus, everyone has a peaceful existence. This isn't to say that a golden retriever is unhappy learning; they love it. But some people just aren't interested in teaching. Even if that is the case, there are at least five commands you are going to want to teach your golden retriever in order to make life easier. We'll start with the basics before learning a couple of entertaining tricks to teach.

Come:

GOLDEN RETRIEVER

You might use another word, but the end goal is the same; we want our golden retriever over by us. Maybe we want to pat them, or just simply keep them from running after a squirrel. Regardless of the reason, this is the number one command that our dogs need to learn. It isn't very hard to teach this one. Get yourself a nice long rope and attach it to the dog's collar. Keep it in hand and walk a little ways away, then command the dog to come. If he doesn't, then give the rope a tug. Not enough to hurt your puppy, but enough to get them moving towards you. Repeat this, giving a treat whenever they properly come. Once the dog starts to come immediately, you can remove the rope and start practicing it without it. It is very important to give your dog treats when it obeys. But, it is also important not to be too rough, as we don't want to harm the dog in any way. When first learning this command, the puppy may find it uncomfortable. Remember that this is confusing to them; give them lots of love and play after the training session finishes.

GOLDEN RETRIEVER

Sit:

While there are many reasons to get your dog to sit, the biggest reason is that it helps to calm them down. If you are out in public with your golden retriever and it starts to want to go running off after something, you can use "Sit" to stop it in its tracks. Of course, in public, you should have your dog on a leash, and so be close enough to keep it sitting. When you aren't as close, a dog is more likely to ignore the command. It isn't that they are willfully disobedient, but rather they get caught up in their play like silly kids. You can teach your golden retriever to sit by making the command a part of supper. Once the dog understands that the food bowl is where it eats, you can begin teaching it to sit before you feed it. Holding the bowl, push the dog's butt down while you say sit. At first, the dog will be too excited about the forthcoming food to listen to you. But, as it realizes you want something, it will start to follow along. Once the dog sits on its own, you put down the food bowl and let them eat. This makes teaching sit super-easy, but you need to be careful to make sure it doesn't just stay a supper time command. Once they understand sit, you need to use the command in other locations and at different times. Make sure that you use treats at these points so that the connection between response and reward are reinforced. When you forget to use treats, sitting becomes a less significant command outside of the supper time ritual.

Stay:

Stay is another command that can be taught using the supper time ritual. Remember to work on one command at a time this way. Start with sit, then move to stay. Learning to sit first will make this much easier. Have the dog sit, and then place the food dish far enough away so that the dog would have to get up and walk over to it. Make sure you tell it to stay as you place it down. If it starts to move, pick up the dish, and try again. You may want to add a physical component to the command, such as a hand signal, so as to make it very clear to the dog that you are trying to teach it a command. If your golden retriever is a quick learner, then they might catch onto this the first time. However, a dog that is slow to catch on shouldn't be trained this way with their supper. You shouldn't deprive the dog of a meal because it failed to catch onto a command. Therefore, you should still be placing the bowl down and giving them the food even when the lesson was a failure. If they don't catch on the first time, then use a treat to teach stay, and try again with supper later on. Also, make sure that you keep the dog sitting for various lengths of time. We want them to listen to this command and stay until we say it is okay. If we always make them stay for only five seconds, then they may grow to think of this duration as part of the command as well. By switching up the length, you make it clear to the dog that only you can tell them when it is time to go.

Kennel:

Not used nearly as often, this one is still useful to know. It is also better to learn this earlier since you will use it more for a puppy then you will for a grown dog. Being able to command a dog into its kennel makes it much easier to travel, and it can be used to settle down an excited dog if you have to put them away for any particular reason. Whenever you put your dog into the kennel, say, "Kennel." Give them a small treat, as well. This will help to comfort them and make them feel less scared about the experience. You should also provide them with a favorite toy, especially if they aren't used to the kennel yet. Saying kennel as you put them in will start to make the connection. After a couple of times, start just saying kennel, and rewarding the dog when they get in themselves. Confined spaces can be frightening experiences for a dog, but, by giving them a treat and reinforcing the kennel as a safe place, you can make it a positive experience for your golden retriever.

No:

This is the command that every single dog should know. It is a very straightforward one. Always say it with a loud, deep voice. More than any word, the sound itself carries disappointment and disapproval. It is very easy for a dog to understand what this command means. Simply put, the dog hears no and immediately knows it should stop whatever it is doing because something is wrong. Golden retrievers are especially good at following this command because they absolutely hate to disappoint their special human. Any behavior that you want to cut out needs to be addressed with a no. If the dog isn't allowed on the couch? Don't only say no after they jump on, but say it when you spot them even thinking about it. If they aren't allowed to jump up and lick your guests, then, rather than tell them "down," use a firm no. They won't know the word "down," and most of the time, we don't reward them even if they do listen. But a strong no is easy to understand, and they will immediately see they have to stop. The crucial part is to make sure that your voice is clear and direct. You don't want to be giggling while saying, "No, stop." You need to be clear so that there can be no way for the dog to misunderstand.

Clean Up:

When golden retrievers are young, they have a lot in common with kids. Both golden retrievers and children seem to own a thousand toys, and neither one knows how to tidy them up. While I can't help you with your children, there is hope for your golden retriever. First off, get yourself a basket for the dog's toys. The secret here is first to teach your dog what its toys are called. Whenever you play with the dog, tell it the name of the toy you are playing with. Hold it up, say the name, then play with the dog. Over time, you will be able to say the name of the toy, and the dog will run and pick it up. Make sure you reward this behavior with a treat, and get this trick in place. Once the golden retriever knows all of its toys, you can start teaching it how to clean up. Stand next to the basket you purchased and dangle a treat above it. When you have its attention, name the toy you want. Since the dog badly wants that treat, you might be shocked at how quickly you get the toy you wanted. Instead of taking it, instruct the dog to drop the toy into the basket. Once the toy is successfully dropped into the basket (and not just around the basket), then you can hand over a treat. Repeat this process until every toy has been put away. When the last toy is tidied away, don't just give the dog that treat, but provide them with an even bigger one while saying "clean up" or something to that effect. It will take some time, but this is a terrific bit of training that can provide you with an extra hand for cleaning up around the house. While it starts with the dog's toys, you can extend this training to many different items for giving you a hand fetching and tidying.

Considering Clicker Training

Clicker training is done by using a device that makes a clicking noise. When you are teaching a dog a command, you can use a clicker as an alternative way to give instructions. You first introduce your dog to the clicker, then you use the clicker whenever it is making the desired response, and you immediately follow the noise with a treat. By teaching the dog that the click is a command, you can use this as a way of training instead of just verbal commands. However, clicker training is consistently more effective when it is used with praise for positive reinforcement. While there are people who swear by it, there isn't a lot of hard evidence that it's a more effective method. Rather than a better solution to the classic approaches, clicker training is an alternative. We'll take a quick look at what people like about it before we move onto discipline and reinforcement in the next chapter, but it is useful to understand that both classic training and clicker training are perfectly valid ways of training. Pick the approach that is right for you and your circumstances.

Those owners that enjoy clicker training claim that it is a more accurate way to provide your dog with feedback. It is useful for your dog to understand which behavior it is you are praising. If you are trying to teach them to sit, and they sit and then lay down, they may not know if the sitting or the laying down was the thing they received praise for. You use a clicker the second the dog does the right behavior, and this lets them know precisely what it is you're pleased with. Plus, once a dog gets to know this, then they often find it quite fun. While anthropomorphizing your dog isn't a good idea, it's hard not to see the joy and happiness in their face once they get the hang of this kind of training.

Another benefit of clicking training is that it can start much sooner than you could otherwise. Clicker training works in a more straightforward manner than traditional practice does in that there is a singular sound that marks success and commands, instead of a whole bunch of different commands and words used for praise. While these are in no way bad, they are more information for a puppy to figure out compared to a single click. This makes it a much simpler method for the puppies to understand, as well as children. If you have kids, then clicker training can be a great way to teach them the basics of training a puppy with ease. Plus, fans of clicker training argue that using it will help you to improve your training skills in general. This is true as it follows the same pattern as traditional training, but it is done in a more streamlined fashion. That means the teacher can get more deeply involved in the process of instruction itself, as opposed to the frustration that often accompanies the training of any new skill for the first time.

This simplicity of use makes adding a clicker to just about any training problem a hassle-free experience. Most training requires you to have a treat to give the dog, and this is still true with the clicker training, but you can use the clicker as a way to train anywhere you want. Taking the dog to go pick up the kids? Try using the clicker in the parking lot for some surprise training. Just don't forget to give them a treat later on if they did a good job. As the training sets in fully, you'll be able to leave the clicker behind eventually. It is a tool that is used for training; it is not the source of the commands or the knowledge. But it does work as a way of positive reinforcement to make the experience a positive one for the dog. We'll look more at discipline and positive reinforcement in the following chapter.

GOLDEN RETRIEVER

Chapter Summary

- Golden retrievers started as hunting dogs, but they are smart enough to be useful in many different fields of employment.

- Golden retrievers take well to training because they love pleasing their owners and following directions.

- You will want to train your golden retriever yourself. Your bond will make it more likely for the dog to listen, and you'll know for sure that they listen to you and not just the trainer you hired.

- It is better to start training them when they're young so they can learn more before adolescence.

- The best way to train a golden retriever is to teach them what you want through physical and verbal commands, rewarding the right behavior with treats.

- Treats and play are brilliant ways to reward a dog.

- The most important commands to teach a golden retriever are come, sit, stay, kennel, and no!

- Clean up is a fun command that gets your dog to remember the name of objects in the house.

GOLDEN RETRIEVER

You'll teach your golden retriever how to tidy up its toys, but this same process can be used to teach all sorts of things such as fetching the newspaper in the morning.

- Clicker training uses a clicking sound tool to help reinforce positive behavior in your dog. Many trainers claim that clicker training is better than traditional training. While this is up to personal preference, it can be a powerful tool in helping you educate your dog.

- Clicker training can let you start teaching your golden retriever while it is still younger than traditional methods require. That can give you a head start. It can also be a lot of fun for your golden retriever and serve as a bonding experience for you both.

In the next chapter, you will learn how to discipline your golden retriever. Discipline is one of those words with a negative connotation, but you'll see that we want to stay far away from the negative side of discipline. Instead, when working with your golden retriever, you will want to focus on positive reinforcement. You'll learn why this is and how to do it before the end of the next section.

CHAPTER SEVEN

HOW TO DISCIPLINE YOUR GOLDEN RETRIEVER

Training your golden retriever is a lot of fun, though it will also require a lot of patience from you. The central fact is that you understand the right way to discipline your golden retriever. It's by positive reinforcement. Your golden retriever will want to please you, but they need to be given time to understand what's needed.

Unfortunately, many people don't want to give this process the time that is required, and so they try to speed it up by using fear and abuse to teach their dogs. This behavior is disgusting, but it does lead to results, and so people continue using it. But dogs trained through fear often develop anxiety or aggressive behavior. You could cause your dog a lifetime of suffering just to teach them not to jump on the couch. Doesn't really seem worth it, does it?

We're not going to get any deeper into fear-based discipline except to point out that a stern "No!" command is not a fear response. This is a command, never a threat. If you need to discipline your golden retriever, then you will want to learn about the power of reinforcement.

What is Reinforcement and Why Does it Work?

Reinforcement is one of the most powerful psychological tools we have. Note, I didn't say "that we have for our dogs." Reinforcement is a psychological tool that we can use to train ourselves as well as dogs. If we use reinforcement on ourselves, then we are developing what is called "neuroplasticity." This is the rewiring of the brain itself. Studies are still being carried out to see if it true that "you can't teach an old dog new tricks," but we've learned for sure this isn't true of humans. We do know that dogs learn best when they start young, but this is the same with humans, so there is a very high chance that neuroplasticity is happening in your dog's brain all the time.

To make this a little easier to understand, the information in the brain is like the trees in the forest. If you want to get to a specific tree, then you need to find it. If there are well-trodden paths through the grass to get there, the journey is simple. As you train your dog, you are planting new trees in this forest, and you are teaching them how to get there. You want them to create the fastest, easiest pathway so that when you say "Sit," they immediately find the "sit tree" and plant their furry butts on the ground. When the tree is new, the dog doesn't know how to get there. These trees include commands like "sit," "stay," and "No!" but also things like "don't sit on the couch" or "wait patiently for supper instead of knocking mommy over." You know exactly which of these trees you want your dog to find, but you need to be careful how you discipline it to get the lesson across.

If you are mean and frightening, then you are going to make the pathway to that tree dark and scary. It's going to be worse than any horror movie you've ever watched. The dog will learn what you intend, but the way is horrifying and cruel. Using fear as reinforcement creates fearful dogs. That's the thing, using fear and threats against a dog is simply another form of reinforcement. Any time you get the dog to walk through a chain of behavior, then you are reinforcing that behavior. Fear and threats are negative, but they are not what is meant by negative reinforcement. These habits are negative reinforcement taken to the extreme of abuse, and there is no excuse for this. It only plants sick and infected trees in the forest of your dog's mind.

If we want our dogs to be healthy of mind and happy in life, then we need to use techniques of positive reinforcement. When your golden retriever sits after you give the command, give them a treat. This treat is a positive reinforcement. Scientists have found that the mind has a firm connection to the stomach. That is why the way to a dog's heart is through giving it something to eat. They are suckers for a treat. Giving a reward as they learn a technique helps them to learn the command because it is positive reinforcement. The cycle they go through is: **stimulus + response = reward**. They need to learn each part of this for it to work. But you need to provide each part. If there is no reward, then there is merely stimulus and response. If they respond to sit by sitting, but then they lay down next time, they have no idea which behavior was right if you didn't provide them with a treat for positive reinforcement. Fun fact, using sugary treats in this manner helps humans to develop habits too.

Negative reinforcement is pretty much giving your dog a time out. Go sit in the corner doesn't work particularly well with a golden retriever, but you could remove a toy or something as a punishment. Negative reinforcement is produced by taking something away from the dog. Denying the dog something that it enjoys. Just make sure that you don't deny the dog your love, food, water, medicine, or exercise. These aren't luxuries, they are requirements for the dog's health, and this would just be cruel. You can deny the dog your attention, refuse to pet or reward it, and perhaps focus yourself on a television show or a book. Just remember that when you finally do give your attention, or give the toy back to the dog, that this is a positive reward; you need to make sure you're sending the right message and not caving in to its entreaties.

Using reinforcement to train your dog requires patience and understanding, but it takes into account the way the dog's mind needs to grow and develop over time. Positive behavior is rewarded, and, with time, you can train a dog that is as obedient as they are loyal and adorable.

GOLDEN RETRIEVER

GOLDEN RETRIEVER

Chapter Summary

- It takes a lot of time and effort to train a golden retriever (or any dog), and you may want to make this experience faster. Using fear or physical violence as a way to discipline your golden retriever is a terrible method and one that no owner should ever practice.

- There is no shortcut in training your dog, unfortunately. But by understanding how reinforcement and the brain works, you can understand how your actions train your dog both consciously and unconsciously.

- Firm commands like "No!" are not using fear. At no point does "No!" imply that you are going to follow through with violence against the dog.

- Reinforcement is the act of rewarding a behavior so that it happens again. By giving a treat or something to your dog when they obey, you teach them that this behavior gets a reward. When they do it a second time, they get a second reward, and it is reinforced.

- At the same time, by walking through a behavior over and over, you reinforce the behavior within the dog's mind so that it is easier for the dog to listen and follow. This reinforces the behavior itself.

- By reinforcing the behavior with a reward and reinforcing the behavior neurologically by repeating the routine, you train your dog in the best way possible.

- Using fear and physical violence to train a dog might get the dog to follow the command, but it does so through dark neurological places. By using positive reinforcement, you make the behavior something that the dog wants to do instead of something it is forced to do.

- There are a lot of connections between the brain and the stomach, and so using food as positive reinforcement is a powerful tool. You can also use extra walks, car rides, or playtime as rewards.

- Negative reinforcement means to take away something from the dog as a punishment. If it's chewing a lot of things, then you'd take away its favorite wishbone.

- Remember that giving back the wishbone is a positive sign to the dog, so try to think about the lesson you are sending. Be careful about the time and context you give back any toys or restore anything taken away as a part of negative reinforcement.

In the next chapter, you will learn the timeline of a golden retriever. From puppy to adolescence, adolescence to adulthood, these dogs will continue to grow, change, and mature. You'll learn to understand the signs of their age and what you can expect from each step along their path through life.

CHAPTER EIGHT

TIMELINE OF A GOLDEN RETRIEVER

In this chapter, we're going to take a quick look at what you can expect out of the three stages of your golden retriever's growth. As a puppy, it is going to be up to you to be careful about their safety and mindful of their needs. This is also going to be the best point at which to train a golden retriever so that you can get some instructions in before they become a naughty little adolescent furball. In adolescence, your golden retriever isn't going to be a nightmare, but they're going to be harder to train and keep in line, so you'll need to watch out. But this doesn't last long before you have yourself an adult golden retriever.

GOLDEN RETRIEVER

Golden Retriever Puppies (0-1.5 years)

Retrievers remain as puppies for roughly a year and a half. Towards the end of that period, they will also become an adolescent. That latter stage is the interim between the end of being a puppy and the start of being an adult. It always happens, but it never quite seems to hit at the same time for any two dogs.

Puppies are going to get bigger and bigger throughout this time. They open their eyes two weeks after they are born, and then they start to walk a week later. Somewhere between when they start walking and the end of their first month being alive, they grow teeth and start eating more like a normal dog. If you are getting

GOLDEN RETRIEVER

a new puppy, then your golden retriever will be somewhere between two and three months old, and you will want to begin training them as soon as they are comfortable with you and their new home.

If you find that your puppy keeps you up all night like a cat, then they are probably a little bit younger. Around four months of age, they start sleeping through the night, and you won't have to get up as much. Tiny bodies need to go out to pee more often, and the dog can't help this fact. Around this time, you might notice that your dog isn't chewing on things nearly as much. You might also be horrified to discover its teeth falling out. There is no need to worry. Dogs lose their baby teeth just the way that we did. Their adult teeth will come in, and it will be okay.

Your next big checkmark is around a year old. After this point, your golden retriever is going to be about as tall as it is ever going to get. Changes happening at this point are going to be a little bit more subtle. Their coat will fill out, and they'll keep putting on weight for a while as their muscles and organs mature and grow thick and strong. At two months of age, a golden retriever puppy will be about 10 pounds. By the end of a year, they may be full weight, but many take two years. Generally, you can expect your puppy to be putting on two or three pounds a week when they are youngest.

GOLDEN RETRIEVER

Adolescent Golden Retrievers (8 months - two years)

Just because they're covered in fur and look like the cutest creature put on this Earth, don't think that your golden retriever puppy will magically skip over adolescence. Every sweet little child will turn into an annoying teenager, and things are no different for golden retrievers. Still, they are quite adorable at this point.

But that cuteness comes primarily from the fact that they are still puppies in a technical sense. You can never be quite sure when adolescence is going to hit since each golden retriever is different. But it really is just the teenage years, so you are still going to feed them us usual, and there is no need to treat them any differently when it comes to their health. But you are going to want to prepare yourself for some adorably frustrating times ahead. The keyword is frustrating, not adorable, unfortunately.

When dogs enter this stage, it's hard to teach them much of anything. You are going to want to start early to get the basics down because an adolescent golden retriever is going to mess around and pretend it's forgotten the training. This can become a struggle and might make you want to give up, but you need to stick through the training and keep going, or you will lose it here. You will be doing brilliantly at training your puppy, and then, suddenly, it will seem like all the progress just vanished. You shouldn't give up. Soldier on through and continue reinforcing the positive behavior when it happens.

During this stage, there is also going to be a lot of extra shedding. Puppies have their special coat of fur, and they need to get rid of this so they can grow in that beautiful double coat of theirs. Revisit chapter four for steps on how to make this experience easier on yourself when it comes to cleaning, and coping with the walking explosion of dog hair that is your golden retriever during this stage.

Get lots of chew toys so that your golden retriever can learn how to use its adult teeth. You might also notice that your puppy is falling a lot and seems to have lost much of its dexterity. This is perfectly normal; the puppy's legs are growing faster than it has learned how to use them. These tumbles and accidents are just part of growing into an adult and learning how to control a bigger body.

During these years, your puppy might also mark territory by peeing on it if it is male. If the golden retriever is female, then she will be going into her first heat at some point. Much like a teenager with hormones pumping through their body, your dog is the same way. You might notice they become a little moody. They're growing, and not every part of growing is comfortable. Because of this shift in mood, a lot of people slow down on introducing their adorable puppy to new people and animals. Despite this temporary teenage attitude, you should keep introducing your puppy to new people so that it develops into an adult that has no problem meeting new family members or friends wherever they go.

GOLDEN RETRIEVER

Adult Golden Retrievers (2 years - 12 years)

We've pretty much already covered adult golden retrievers throughout this book. Adolescence will eventually fade away into adulthood, the same way that teenagers eventually realize they don't need to fight against life all the time. From around two years of age, you have yourself a golden retriever that is fully grown and should be between 65 and 75 pounds if they are a male, and 55 to 65 pounds if they are a female. They're pretty large dogs, and they're going to shed twice a year.

They're also going to be prone to health problems and require a lot of exercise. You will need to appreciate that a golden retriever may be an expensive family member to have. Health care costs money, and exercise requires time. But if you can offer these to your golden retriever, then you may be able to spend a wonderful decade together with a tremendous canine pal.

After adolescence, golden retrievers begin to settle down in their adulthood. That doesn't mean they don't still get excited or hyper occasionally. We all do that throughout life from time to time, and our golden retrievers are no different. But they are wise dogs that are eager to please, enjoy helping their masters, and meeting new friends and family. If you have trained them well, then an adult golden retriever can be a more productive companion than some of the co-workers you've seen over the years!

Health issues become more common the older a golden retriever gets, and you can expect them to pass somewhere around ten to twelve years. Many live longer, but unfortunately, these sweet-natured creatures are having a hard time at the moment. But ten years is a long time to have a best friend, and, if you're lucky, it might just be a whole lot longer.

Chapter Summary

- Golden retrievers are puppies for the first year and a half. During this period, you can expect them to put on a few pounds every week as they grow.

- At some point, your golden retriever puppy will enter their adolescence and start to act a little bit differently, this is perfectly routine, and it is a sign that your puppy is becoming a teenager.

- Puppies open their eyes after two weeks and get their baby teeth around three to four weeks.

- At two or three months, a golden retriever is ready to be adopted into its new home.

- Puppies have small bodies, and so little bladders and bowels. That means they will need to go out often, and they won't be able to sleep through a whole night until month four.

- Around month four, you might also find some of the puppy's teeth. Puppies must lose their baby teeth to make room for their adult teeth. Puppies chew on everything while they are dealing with their new teeth, so you should have a few chew toys on hand to help make this less painful.

- Around a year of age, a golden retriever will be as tall as they get. They might be at full weight,

- Adolescence for golden retrievers starts sometime after their eighth month, and it can last anywhere up to the second year. These are the teenage years for your golden retriever.

- Adolescents will be harder to train than puppies, so you want to make sure you start teaching your golden retriever as soon as possible. Adolescent golden retrievers may act like they have forgotten their training and cause you lots of frustration. Stick with it to show them there is no room for bad behavior.

- Golden retrievers will become more territorial and moody during this time. Nonetheless, you should keep introducing your golden retriever to new people and socializing them so that they grow into properly functioning adults.

- Golden retrievers become adults around the time they are two. They should be between 55 to 75 pounds, depending on their sex. They are going to be loving dogs that require lots of exercise to stay healthy.

- Golden retrievers are prone to health problems, so you shouldn't be surprised if your dog experiences some. That's one of the unfortunate issues with adult golden retrievers, and it keeps their life expectancy around 10 to 12 years.

GOLDEN RETRIEVER

- Adult golden retrievers are far more peaceful and calm than adolescent golden retrievers. Puppies are adorable, and adults are calm, but adolescents can be a stressful experience. Comfort yourself by knowing that it ends almost as quickly as it begins.

FINAL WORDS

Golden retrievers are among the most intelligent breeds there are when it comes to our canine friends. Some golden retrievers even hold jobs more complicated than what you or I do for a living. These wonderful creatures may have been hunting dogs initially, but they have a depth of compassion that makes them terrific additions to any family. Some dogs may get jealous at the attention its owners give to a toddler, but a golden retriever will love the toddler just as much as the parents do. They are truly kind and gentle souls, and you now have everything you need to know in order to introduce a golden retriever into your family.

You will need to remember the responsibility that a puppy brings. They need to be taught commands, taught what they're allowed to chew on and what they're not, taught where to pee and when. Everything that a dog needs to know, you are going to be teaching your puppy. This takes time and energy, but it will be a rewarding process in the end. Remember that adolescent dogs are going to be more frustrating to deal with, but this is only a short stage your puppy goes through before becoming an adult. We covered training in chapter six, discipline in chapter seven, and a timeline of a golden retriever's growth in chapter eight so that you know how to train yours properly, and when to expect the most difficulty.

We covered health and grooming in chapters four and five. While grooming is mostly done for aesthetic and hygienic reasons, it can and should also be considered a part of keeping your golden retriever healthy. There are a lot of different ailments that you've read about in chapter five, and can now keep an eye out for. One of the easiest ways to do this is to take the required time to groom your golden retriever. The short time you spend doing this will let you keep their coat in perfect condition, reduce the likelihood of illness due to dirt and grime, plus it will help you check for signs of health issues as well as bonding with your dog. So long as you practice the advice in these chapters, you will be able to keep your golden retriever in good shape while getting an early jump on any medical issues that crop up along the way.

It is my deepest hope that you bring a golden retriever into your family and see the joy and happiness they can bring into your lives. Just make sure that you have considered all these needs and are able to provide them for your dog. They are family, after all, and so they should be treated as such. But I know you'll do exactly that.